Last Poems

John Farris

The editors would like thank Phoebe Farris, Chinyelu Farris Duxbury, Mia Hansford, Sienna Farris, Richard Dye, NYU Fales Library John Farris Archive, Maggie Wrigley, Nadia Coen, as well as *Sensitive Skin* and the anthology *Unpublishable* (Archway Editions, 2020) where portions of this book were first published.

Published in the United States by:
Archway Editions, a division of powerHouse Cultural Entertainment, Inc.
32 Adams Street
Brooklyn, NY 11201
www.archwayeditions.us

Daniel Power, CEO
Chris Molnar, Founder and Editorial Director
Nicodemus Nicoludis, Founder and Managing Editor
Naomi Falk, Senior Editor
Mia Risher, Publicist

Edited by Chris Molnar and Nicodemus Nicoludis with Andrew Castrucci
Proofread by Sylvana Widman

Library of Congress Control Number: 2024940490

ISBN: 9781648230509

Printed by Toppan

First edition, 2025

10 9 8 7 6 5 4 3 2 1

Cover image: John Farris, *Untitled Self-Portrait*

Printed and bound in China

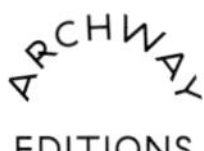

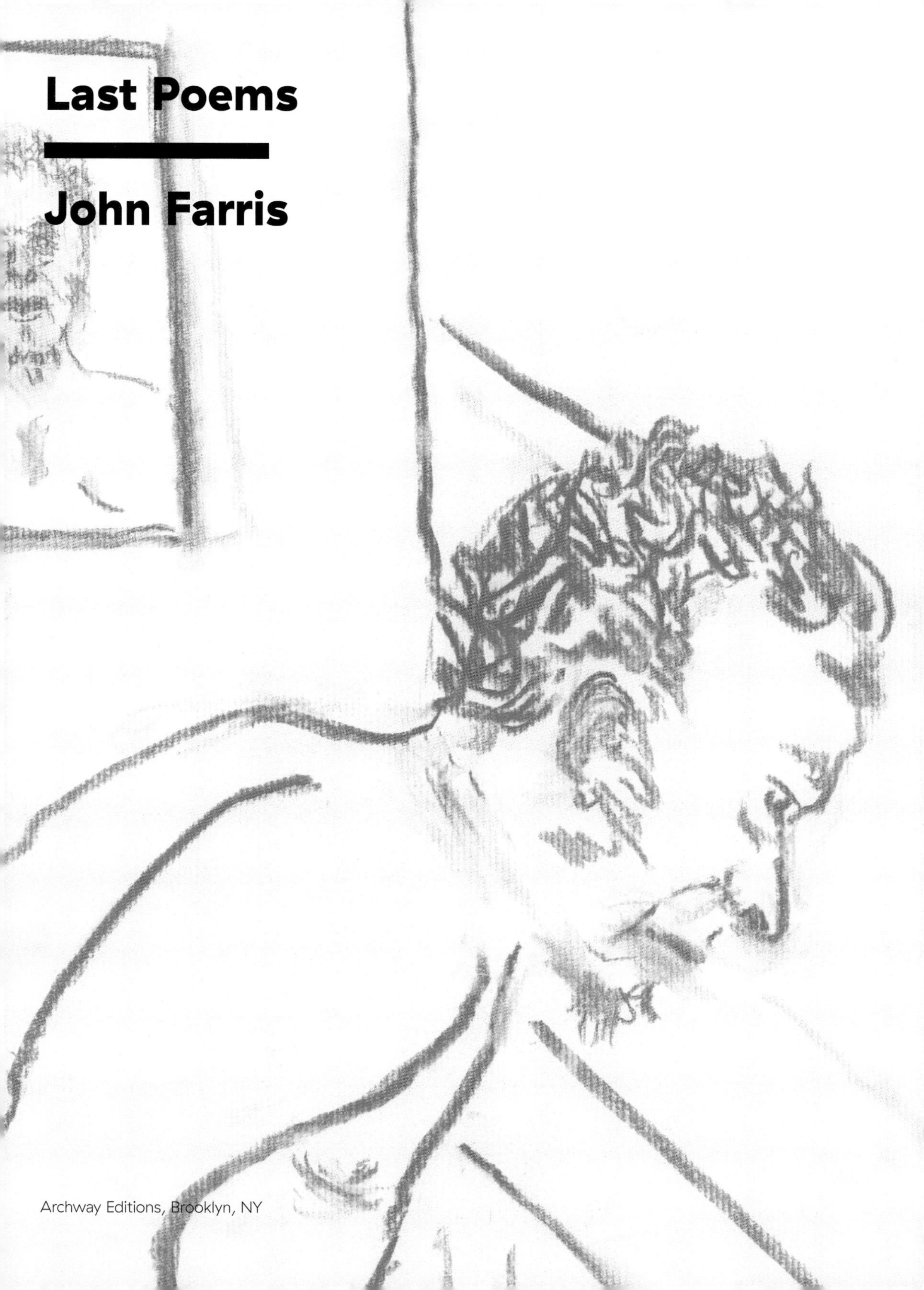

Last Poems

John Farris

Archway Editions, Brooklyn, NY

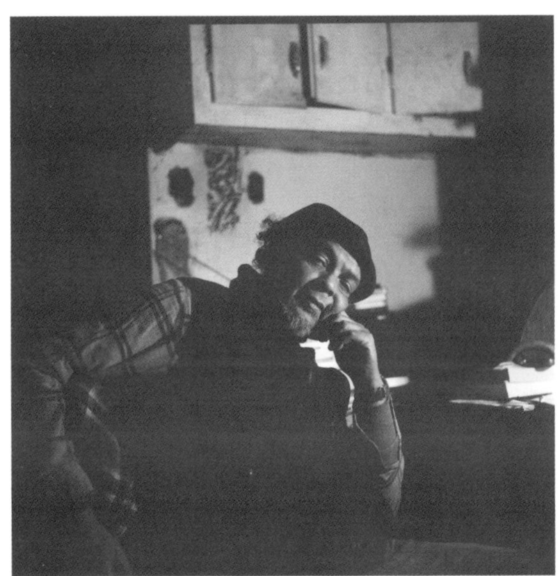

Maggie Wrigley, *John Farris at Bullet Space*, 2009

John Farris, a cantankerous but prolific man of letters, was a casualty of the country's pot prohibition who was later swept into the net of conspiracy that ultimately murdered Malcolm X. He was then shunned by the Black Arts Movement (until all was forgiven in Amiri Baraka's basement). In the end, John was loved, supported, and sustained by the Lower East Side's community of artists and activists, hustlers and freaks, underworld creeps, and dope-snorting elites.

As prickly as he sometimes was, John was a profoundly wise man. I once watched him more than hold his own in a discussion on the writing of Italo Calvino with the wickedly smart Kathy Acker. But the moment etched indelibly in memory for me is the night he stood in the center of Tompkins Square Park, surveying the night with Norman Douglas and I, and announced:

"We are the last Black men..."

This collection is John's output during his final days at Bullet Space. With a joint angled between his lips and a plate of rice and beans from Casa Adela at his elbow, John stared intently into a mirror and endlessly produced a stream of graphite self-portraits on porous paper as he did poetry. Read and be elevated.

DARIUS JAMES

CONTENTS

Editor's Note

The work here represents some of the last poems and drawings John Farris created while living in Bullet Space, a squat-turned-co-op on 3rd Street between Avenue C and D. Visual artist and Bullet co-founder Andrew Castrucci knew him for over thirty years on the downtown art scene; we, only toward the end of his life. John was a living link to an ageless bohemian East Village, still meandering along 3rd Street dispensing wisdom on the stairwell, showing his art in the gallery downstairs, an *éminence grise* still talking shit at Gathering of the Tribes, at Bowery Poetry Club. After he died, Andrew was tasked with keeping and organizing the pages and pages of poems, stories, drawings, and correspondence that decorated Farris' spartan apartment, eventually coming up with the idea for a book of last poems.

Chris (who also lived in Bullet Space for some years) and Nic spent over eight years going through the texts, whenever time allowed, combing through them, transcribing Farris' hard-to-read scribble, using his old typescripts as Rosetta Stones, projecting scans on the wall and going letter by letter, separating his drawings from those drawn of him, for him. Slowly, a book took shape, many books. From his ample archive of works in progress, we discovered the poems and drawings from his last decade or so, all hand-scrawled on computer paper, on the backs of envelopes, of bills, with lists and phone numbers alongside drafts. Filling the top floors with weed smoke, John poured himself into these works, finding inspiration in a lifetime lived as a poet of the people, in the friends he made along the way, the views from his window. At the same time, with the encouragement of his long-time friend David Hammons, John created his masking tape head sculptures in a stroke of thrifty genius to try and make some money.

These are some of his best work, short and elegiac but with the unexpected wit and sharpness and kaleidoscopic frame of reference typical of Farris. We hope this is the first of many books that doubtless will appear from his unpublished, uncollected work, a lifetime's worth written in defiance of the bullshit, searching for the real, unwritten truth—as one poem goes, in its entirety:

> some-
> thing's out
> there—aft (her
> the uni-
> verse). The verse
> is yet.

CHRIS MOLNAR AND NICODEMUS NICOLUDIS

John's Last Poems

This book is a collection of poems John Farris wrote in the last five years of his life. It is also a visual book of John's drawings and sculptures that he began to make around 2006. His visual work was a companion to his writing, and in the last few years of his life, John could not tell the difference between his poems and drawings. You will see. Drawings began to contain text. Poems began to contain scribbles, then actual drawings. For John, the two forms became one. And this convergence seemed to affect his creative process. The poems changed. Before John passed away on January 16, 2016, most of his poems had become short as haikus.

His work is filled with the urban icons of downtown New York: a pile driver in his backyard hammering fifty-foot foundation poles; the bark on a maple tree; the doves nesting on his fire escape; a woman bathing across from his window; a five-year-old kid running above his ceiling like a drum beat; and women from the shelter next door smoking in the alleyway.

On the fourth floor of Bullet Space on East 3rd Street was John's chair with a single light bulb above his desk. This was where he mostly stayed during the last five years of his life, almost as though he knew he was going to leave us and had a lot of work left to do. Some mornings he might take a small stroll to see Gathering of the Tribes at Steve Cannon's across the street or around the corner to hear some music at NUBLU, but John traveled little these last years.

When I remember him and his space, his way of inhabiting his space, and its relationship to his work, Van Gogh's painting of his studio chair or shoes comes to mind. John's chair and desk and light were magical like that—they were filled with his determination and exactitude. John wrote some great work here. His whole life rotated around this chair. It is here that he also created portraits of his friends and portraits of his daughters, whom he missed dearly. Slowly piling up like sculptures themselves were portraits of faces he passed on the street. There are portraits of local musicians who he would gregariously admire and harass, sometimes in the same breath. John had an amazing memory for faces. He would study your features and return home that day and draw your face in solitude. He drew himself as well. John did more self-portraits than Van Gogh. His enormous stack of drawings is ten years' worth of work.

In John's later years, after seeing hundreds of John's self-portraits, David Hammons encouraged him to draw to make a few bucks to survive since writing wasn't enough. Very few people can master two art forms. But John did!

Watching him sculpt plastic bag heads in the last years, I came to believe that these sculptures wrapped in masking tape were his best work. However, having recently gone through thousands of drawings, I am stunned by their expressive power and Art Brut style. John Farris, the exacting poet as an artist, could draw and handle materials deftly and with surprising turns, combining words with images like an Expressionist mix of a *New Yorker* cartoon and a Basquiat.

John is considered a jazz poet in the spirit of John Coltrane and Thelonius Monk, but he had many other influences growing up as a Beat poet with LeRoi Jones, known in his later life as Amiri Baraka. Phoebe Farris (John's second wife) always mentioned John's Seminole mother. John's sensitivity to nature and the curve of the world reflects his connections to his maternal roots. You can see it all over his poetry: in "birds heading south / magnolia trees / the world blue in one eye, in the other, technicolor."

John transcends Realism. John is a deeply American poet—and a modern Romantic. Moreover, he loved the work of the Impressionists and Luminist painters. From Albert Pinkham Ryder to Frederic Church to Casper David Friedrich to the Ashcan School to trends in hip-hop slam poetry—he would bounce off all of them. I can just hear "Cranky Franky" saying, "We invented rap in the 1950s-60s way before these young bloods."

In his last poems, he was drawing with words:

AT LAST

At last
I am
Making
Self-portraits
I can
Get myself
Arrested for.
The bridge
of the nose
will finally take me
to Brooklyn
& back on
positive
identification. It
Balances
The sneer
Of the lips.
The eyes
Look you straight
In the face
With
pure arrogance. Yes—I confess—again,

John's drawings were poems.

And his poems were drawings.

Some days, I still knock on John's door thinking he's home. We were each other's anchor as we navigated the harsh conditions of living in a squat. We turned an uninhabitable building into our home and our sanctuary for writing poems and making art. Burning wood for twenty years to stay warm, burning your eyebrows from getting too close to the electric heater—these were daily moments we both knew.

John lived at Bullet Space for twenty-five years. The first twelve and a half years I couldn't walk past his door without him reading me something; the next twelve and a half years, it became, "Hey Andrew, do these hands look right"…"I'm having trouble with his nose"; "Where's that book *Drawing on the Right Side of the Brain*, I want to borrow it." John was a self-taught artist truly. An American Impressionist in writing and drawing. He recorded not just the old, dark Lower East Side landscape. In both his poems and his drawings, he was a romantic visionary, turning the simplest forms of daily life into poetry. One day, John knocked on my door, screaming that a plane had just hit the Twin Towers; we watched the towers fall from our roof that day.

We sought each other out. We both thought about leaving many times for greener pastures, and we always begged each other not to leave. The building would fall apart!

He was my teacher, and I was his teacher. "How do I make those hands right?" he would ask. I'd reply, "Don't worry John, it's better than Bonnard. Don't try too hard. Stay with your original instincts." Then he'd move to another drawing: "Hey, check out this portrait of Joe Overstreet. Does it look like him?" I would say, "It feels like him. Don't try to be too realistic. Stick to your Art Brut style."

John was the biggest heckler on the Lower East Side, and at one point, he was banned from the Nuyorican Poetry Cafe. Deep down inside, John was a motherfucker—crude, honest, and exacting. At the same time, he could be an extremely sensitive human being. He was a natural teacher and editor. If he liked a young poet, he would generously share his knowledge and his methods. He helped friends edit books. He gave a writing workshop to prisoners. I watched him fight like a bull, swinging his cane, and saw him the next day apologizing in deep sorrow.

Throughout his life, he lived in rough conditions. In the late '80s and early '90s, he took up residence in the basement of The Living Theater. It was an actual living theater for John. In 1992 The Living Theatre's lease was up. John was to become homeless again. That's when I asked him to move into Bullet Space, which at that time was an illegal squat. He lived at Bullet Space for the rest of his life.

Once, we had a fire on the second floor. John made it to the fire escape, but he couldn't climb down the stairs with his bad legs. FDNY Hook and Ladder #11 rescued him; they broke all his windows. After that, I helped John put up plastic over his windows. We nailed down plastic after each major storm while buckets of water collected from the two stories above.

John the warrior poet—his room was so cold it was like sailing over an ocean that winter. But he never complained. He had the lowest electrical bill in the building. He had one light bulb and his desk in the corner and just wrote and drew. John proved to me many times how simple life could be, how tenacious a man could be. That winter, he slept under so many blankets that you couldn't see his head. He said it was like sleeping under a rug. The blankets became so heavy he sometimes had a backache when he awoke.

A French philosopher once said if more than five percent of the public likes your work, you're not an artist. John lived this ethos. Forget your bills, family, wife, lovers, friends. Everybody. John was driven. He was as determined and intrepid as a wolf going after his prey.

Before moving to the Lower East Side, John was Malcolm X's bodyguard from 1964-65. His job was usually to guard Malcolm, but on the day of February 21, 1965, John's duty was switched to guard Betty Shabazz and her children. Also in attendance were John's wife, and his daughter Chinyelu ("Bibi") and her brother. After the assassination, blame was everywhere; John went to Mexico afterward. Before the Lower East Side, John never talked about this time. This was all witnessed and recently discussed with his daughter, Chinyelu Farris Duxbury, who is now living in Mexico.

Before John settled in Harlem in 1959, he went to jail for three years. He was nineteen. He was busted for a single joint of marijuana. While he was serving his time, his mother passed away. He asked for permission to attend her funeral and was denied. In the draconian atmosphere of 1950s America, drug laws were unbelievably strict, especially for a nineteen-year-old Black man.

John Farris was the most famous Unfamous poet alive.

As his legs began to go, John refused to use a walker or wheelchair. At first, he used his bike as a wheelchair; then, when his legs got so bad they would not pedal, he went to crutches. First, on one crutch, then on two. It took him over thirty minutes to get from Avenue C to Avenue B. He never complained about his legs. He just kept writing and drawing and drawing and writing. In the last two years, John would fall a lot. When John fell the whole building shook, and we all knew: John had fallen again. But you couldn't keep this lion down.

One day, I was on a rowboat with John for six hours fishing, drifting with a slow current so peacefully away from New York City for a few days. Most of the time, I got skunked on this lake's highest peak in central New York, but this early October day, we caught so many fish: perch, pickerel, and largemouth bass. One pickerel was a record for this lake: twenty-six inches.

The next day was a little rainy. I was exhausted from the day before. I just wanted to hang out by the river. John said, "Let's go fishing again." He insisted. We went back to the lake and drifted for six more hours, but we caught nothing. As the sun was setting, something amazing happened. Six hundred crows gathered at the top of this mountain. It was an amazing sight. I never saw so many crows in my life. It felt like we were in the middle of a Poe novel or Hitchcock film. Toward the end of his life, John seemed to bring these moments out whenever we would do something. It was as if the crows signaled a last hurrah. A few months later, John left us.

Going through his archive, I wondered how we were going to transcribe all of his handwriting. It will take a lifetime! David Hammons was with me that day, going through John's works, and he said, "We have to leave most of it alone. The beauty of his handwriting is like Japanese calligraphy—the more abstract, the better."

John leaves behind a School of Farris

Farris was the unofficial Lower East Side Poet Laureate. Many artists and writers who were coming into their own and finding their way in the community of artists in the Lower East Side looked to him for his style and his stark editorial choices. He would talk about writing generously and genuinely. They wanted to know who he was reading and why. And he would tell them, saying, "Now, what do you think of that?" Or, "Look how he handles the same guy you were writing about yesterday." He encouraged them to bring the same generosity and sense of deep conversation whenever and wherever—at a bar, in Tompkins Square Park, at a reading event at Saint Marks Church or the Nuyorican, at dinner, at a gallery, at The Stoop. While running an offbeat workshop at Bullet Space with *Sensitive Skin* magazine, I watched a new generation of poets move into the Lower East Side. John was a teacher to them. The way they strolled down the streets, John was like a leader of a gang.

He leaves us six decades of writings, from Harlem to the LES. Readings at Life Cafe, Neither Nor, The Living Theatre, Gathering of the Tribes, the Nuyorican Poets Café, Bob Holman's Bowery Poetry Club, and contributions to *Red Tape Magazine, Between Ave. C & D*, *The Unbearables*, *Peau Sensible/Sensitive Skin*, *TRIBES*, and more.

Emerging writers who sought him out were people like Darius James, Norman Douglas, and Chavisa Woods, to name a few. David Hammons was a close friend and was inspired by John's poetry, as well as by Nathaniel "Junior" Hunter and Steve Cannon. They inspired him deeply, and he loved them. Junior lived on a bench in Tompkins Square Park (during the era of shantytowns in the park). He made glorious installations with found objects. David Hammons, Steve Cannon, and John Farris would hang out near Junior's eclectic mountain and talk. And talk. And plan. This was their common ground. They fed off each other. This is before Steve Cannon's Stoop became a huge scene; and before the Tompkins Square Park riots of 1988.

I observed John slowing down with his writing, even as I admired his obsession with drawing. He would say, "With drawing, I don't have to think." During his last few months, he had a good run, writing many short haikus and fragments about drawing.

This is one of his last pieces:

> Angle. You are
> always after
> some angle… same ol'
> angle; talk about a blast—
> you can't even have
> it straight

Here is the last piece of writing on top of the pile, unfinished:

> draw me
> draw me
> some water
> whatever

From 2016 to 2019, John Farris, Steve Cannon, and Joe Overstreet all left us. The Lower East Side was never the same. In late 2021, David Hammons called and said, "I want you to do a mural of these three artists…I'll pay for the paint, and also, if I have to, I'll pay for the wall. Get your graf artists to help you. Find a good spot, Castrucci."

On 3rd Street and Avenue C, I will occasionally see John hopping down the street on one leg with his cane. John was one of our anchors on the Lower East Side, if not the anchor. American poetry changed when John left us. The world turned upside down—for better or worse.

ANDREW CASTRUCCI

My Father...

My father has been staying with me for the past eight years. It's the longest we've ever lived together, but we don't speak; we are existential roommates, if you will, cohabitating in a brownstone close to the apartment we lived in when I was a baby in Clinton Hill. Life can really be full circle. I see his ashes every morning in my closet; he resides in a sky-blue cardboard box with clouds on it that came from the crematorium. He's so quiet I sometimes forget he's there.

My father had five daughters by four different women, and at the end of his life, only one of them was speaking to him. My father didn't have conversations, he had monologues. He would say, "What's going on in your world?" and before you could even answer he would interrupt you and say, "Do you want to listen to my poem?" And you really had no choice but to say yes. You could be calling him to tell him your arm was falling off, and he wouldn't care. You would just need to take some duct tape, wrap up your arm, and listen to that poem. And then he would read it again and again and again. My father would take out a word and then put it in a new one, or he would read it with a different tempo. He would always ask you what you thought of each iteration of the poem and the right answer was always that you loved it and it was brilliant. And it always was. Even if you didn't understand it, you knew it had to be the best poem you ever heard because my father was a genius. His genius was fueled by his obsession with writing and creating. It was impossible for him to do anything else and that meant that he was incapable of being a reliable father.

My parents split up when I was three, and my mother and I left New York and moved to D.C. He would send us rambling letters that were hard to decipher; hieroglyphics scratched on yellow sheets of legal paper, poems typed on the backs of pages torn out of books. He often wrote about being broke, not having a phone, trying to get published, living in the back of a theater, and missing us. All I have to offer you are my poems, he would write. The letters were sporadic. We sometimes wouldn't hear from him for years. And then he would reemerge. Always something was different. Another tooth missing. A larger belly. A limp. A new scar. He was an alley cat with nine lives.

When he was around, he was indulgent and catered to my whimsy. Writing on the walls was OK. Going for walks at midnight because I didn't feel like sleeping seemed like a perfectly logical plan to him. *You want a puff of my Camel's unfiltered, and you are only five, sure, try it, see if you like it. Come sit at the bar with me. Hey everyone, this is my kid.* He could also be critical. *You dress like a goddamn Jehovah's Witness. What do you mean you don't want a puff of my joint? That's why you're so uptight.*

My father grew up very poor in the projects in the Rockaways. His mother was a single mother with four children, and they often lived in one-room apartments with a bathroom in the hallway. I don't know much about my paternal grandmother. When I asked him what she was like, he said she was very depressed and she liked soap operas. His refuge was the library. He never finished high school. I can't imagine him in that world. He didn't like to talk about that life. He wanted to talk about art, books, politics, and women. And his poems. Always his poems. He didn't truly come alive and into being until he wedded his beloved Loisaida and made his home and community at Bullet Space, biological family be damned.

When I moved back to New York in my twenties, we reestablished our relationship, and at one point we lived just three blocks away from each other. He was amazed that I worked in advertising and even interned at the same agency that turned him down for a copywriting job because they didn't hire Black executives in the *Mad Men* era. Even if they had hired him, he wouldn't have lasted long in corporate America. Some of my earliest memories of my father were seeing him get into fistfights with men. One wrong look or one wrong word, and you would find him rolling around underneath dining room tables or scrapping in between parked cars. As he got older, he didn't have the stamina for fistfights, but his tongue still worked. And his lashings were legendary and cut deep. He burned bridges in the literary and art word, and he burned bridges with me. He was my father again, and then he wasn't, and then he was, and then he wasn't. I wanted more than he could give, and his brilliant poems were not enough for me.

When I found out my father had died, I was eating lunch at one of those miserable Korean delis in Midtown with the fluorescent lighting and the steam buffets. I had just spent my morning in a meeting where my coworkers had spent hours going over the same PowerPoint slides. We had finally gotten a break for lunch, and I remember thinking to myself, "I would do anything to get out of this meeting." And that's right when a policeman called me and told me that my father had died. I remember asking them why they were calling me. And they said because I was the one closest to him. I yelled into the phone that I wasn't closest to him. My sister Bibi was, she was the one who talked to him every day. They should really be calling her. The policeman clarified that he meant physically closer, not emotionally. *Oh,* I said. *You are right. I am the closest.*

SIENNA FARRIS

At Last

At last
I am
Making
Self-portraits
I can
Get myself
Arrested for.

The bridge
of the nose
Will finally take me
To Brooklyn
& back on
positive
Identification. It

Balances
The sneer
Of the lips.

The eyes
Look you straight
In the face
With
pure arrogance. Yes— I confess—again,
I did that. ~~[illegible]~~ – ~~[illegible]~~.
I'm bad.

AT LAST

At last
I am
Making
Self-portraits
I can
Get myself
Arrested for.
The bridge
of the nose
will finally take me
to Brooklyn
& back on
positive
identification. It
Balances
The sneer
Of the lips.
The eyes
Look you straight
In the face
With
pure arrogance. Yes—I confess—again,
I did that.
I'm bad.

BARKING IN BLUE

Here we are again: it's seeing you that brings out
the old canine in me: how you pull me to you like a cat:
I [illegible] at your flat, at you, like a puppy, your toes. You
push me to you, and away. [illegible] I have to sit somewhere, whining.
I suppose being out with you
is like being in the army.
I would be in your company all dog-gone day.
Generally speaking, you give the orders. I run it
up the flagpole, barking in canine, corporal
(or poral), on point, "One day," I say, one day
you'll get it—one day you'll
understand: limits," you
tell me, "limits. (How is that for language.)
that for language.

BARKING IN BLUE

it's seeing you, that brings out
the old canine in me: how you pull me to you like a cat:
I lick at your flat belly, at you like a puppy, your toes. You
push me to you and away. Panting I have to sit somewhere whining.
I suppose being out with you
Is like being in the army.
        in your company all doggoned day
Generally speaking you give the orders. I run
up the flagpole; barking in canine,
corporeal, on point, "one day," I say, one day
you'll get it—one day you'll
understand! "limits," you
tell me, "limits." (How is that for language.)

A friend said
what you draw best
Is triangles, Blacks
& whites,

II

I make it clear
That anybody can
read the colors.

A friend said
what you draw best
Is trouble. Blacks
& whites.

II

I make it clear
that anybody can
have the blues.

AGATE

Friends grapple
With my grapes, my almonds, while I thought
The damned things
Looked almost edible
~~[illegible]~~. One thing that was
~~[illegible]~~, probably an odd angle was something
~~[illegible]~~
Strangest, an old
Girlfriend in my mind I never would get
straight on

A tee shirt
I should stitch with stars
& stripes. They say it's trash.
I say it's supposed to be eggshells,
Something familiar
That suggests the new.

I have to admit
To being pretty green again
& again & yet again,

AGATE

Friends grapple
with my grapes, my almonds, while I [-----].
The damned things
Looked almost edible
          One [-----] what was
probably an odd angle was something
straight, an old
Girlfriend in my mind I never could get
straight or
A tee shirt
I [-----] with stars
& stripes. They say its trash.
I say it's supposed to be eggshells,
something familiar
That suggests the new.

I have to admit
to being pretty green again
& again at agate.

3rd St. Cancan

The corpulence
of dance
shakes it out
like a line in
3rd St. forget
those trendy boots,
we
are talking about here

bodies
with no sweat, pork
and potatoes, bags
of rice, and
hot tomatoes – nothing
prissy, it's
what the heart does –
, , some
ous cumbia, some
cancan for shake
talk about the willies
about Oya
that pipe that
pipe

3RD ST. CANCAN

The corpulance
of dance
shakes out
like a line in
3rd St. forget
those trendy boots
we
are talking about

booties
with no sweat, pork
and potatoes, bags
of rice,
hot tomatoes—nothing
proasic, it's
what the heat does

cumbia, some
cancan for sure
talk about the willies
talk about
that pipe

BLOWN

Attempting a friend passing a tree
I said, I don't – to be
Truthful – really like this drawing much, but
you know what I happen
To like?" ~~[illegible]~~
~~[illegible]~~ "I really like
That tree. It came
From my ~~[illegible]~~ like a nude." The friend
Said he didn't like
Any of it, tree or
Whatever.

BLOWN

Attempting a friend passing a tree
I said, I don't—to be
Truthful—really like this drawing much, but
You know what I happen
To like.
            "I really like
That tree. It came
From my hand like a nude." The friend
Said he didn't like
Any of it, tree or
Whatever

SKUNK

The pot I'm
smoking now
smells like
Armpits after sex (
not with you
of course). You
always tell me
to go to hell. (This
may be the
last time we
see each other.) Where
I will lie is where
I say I loved
you more than this.

TEACHING

once I imagined you

impressed A poet, I thought, how dare was that
by me:
this class! These days
i imagine
myself more a
choreographer
working
at same dance
you're good at
you say its
that line that gives you kick, that

it's that the way.
all I need
is color
in those skirts
those blouses that!
those hats. Imagine you telling me
talking about
my imagination. What I need to do
fix your eyes, your
mouth
something.

TEACHING

Once imagined you
impressed by me: A poet, I thought, how was that
for class! These days
i imagine
myself more a
choreographer
working
at some dance
you're good at
you say it's
the line that gives you kick, that
conga, that rag,
all I need
is color
in those skirts
those blouses
those hats. Imagine that! you telling me
talking about
my imagination, when I need to
fix your eyes, your
mouth, learn melody
get some rhythm

VERSE

some-
thing's out
there—aft (her
the uni-
verse). The verse
is yet.

WORKING

Not a thing I do has any
Amount of permanency. Not a rock
In the ground! Masking tape &

Plastic. Wax material nobody
wants. A promise. I break another! Glasses, pencils,
Pens, all up in smoke, or flat—colorless

unless I add some felt or
Draw in a cap or draw in a hat that's got
To suggest red. I'm what they used to call
The Japanese. What I want
Is not right & it gets
Left. A fan next to a table. What

Was that Durante said?
I teach myself to get the Chinese,
The North & South Koreans. What do I know about rendering
Mongolians in graphite? I
Think I'm so smart, who can tell a peach
From a pear or an orange?

WORKING

Not a thing I do has any
Amount of permanancy. Not a [----]
In the crowd. Masking tape &
Plastic. War materiel nobody
Wants. A promise. I break things: Glasses, pencils,
pens, all up in smoke, or flat-colorless
unless I add some felt or
Drawing a cup or drawing a hat that's got
To suggest red. I'm what they used to call
The Japanese. What I want
Is not right & it gets
Left. A fan next to a table. What
was that Durante said?
I teach myself to get the Chinese,
The North & South Koreans, what do I know about rendering
Mongolians in graphite? I
Think I'm so smart; who can tell a peach
From a pear or an orange?

CALLIT

Tobacco
cotton
sugar in
Louisiana
shifts
made of gingham
and slivers
coffee
and the crack
of what twang of what
tight strings what

on earth under
the sun nothing mngs

but time now
for the
loud coffee
is like that double
time to
the old swing

CALL IT

Tobacco
cotton
sugar in
Louisiana
shirts
made of gingham
and slaves
after
and the crack
of what twang of what
tight strings what
on earth under
the sun nothing mugs
but time
for the
load coffee
is like that double
time to
the old swing

CRAFT

ing

, (when

it comes to 'pops' I tell my grandson

I am

a Louie man,

man, a

johnny dodds, anyway man

. Maybe

getting ahead some bread

in

Kansas (give him

the dope.) I tell him he's got the tune

to let that be something

a lesson to

him, huh? he laughs.

he thinks. he thinks

he knows everything before

he calls

the tune. The sycophant I am

is produced

by what I am.

CRAFT

(when
it comes to 'pops' I tell my grandson
I am
a Louie man,
johnny dodds, dry.
Maybe
after that some band
in Kansas (give him
the dope.) I tell him he's got the tune
to let that be
a lesson to
him, [hemp]? he laughs.
he thinks,
he knows everything before
he calls
the tune. The sycophant I am
is produced
by what I am.

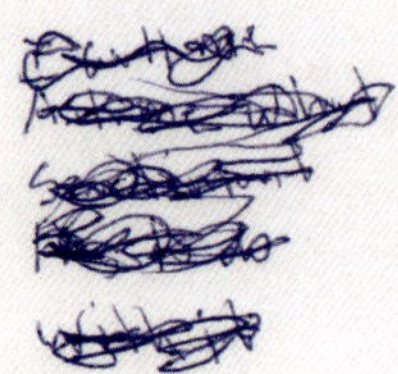
DRAW ME
Draw me
Some water
whatever

DRAW ME

Draw me
some water
whatever

ENFORCEMENT

"I might as well go back to Peoria, N.Y.

is a bum," he said gesticulating wildly.

I saw what he was talking about coming up the block, the captain of the police department fronting a phalanx of minor functionaries from various municipal bureaucracies; the fire department, the health department, the [illegible] of enforcement,

approaching with that confidence / only absolute authority bestows, confidence that brooks no contradiction, compliance; that was what they said [illegible]; and you; you; you

and you too [illegible]; [illegible] [illegible] explain [illegible] that

I know, while [illegible].

ENFORCEMENT

"I might as well go back to Peoria; N.Y.
is a bum," he said gesticulating wildly.
I saw what he was talking about coming
up the block, the captain of the police department
fronting a phalanx of minor functionaries
from various municipal bureaucracies; the fire
department, the health department, hellbent
on enforcement,
approaching with that confidence
only absolute authority bestows confidence that
brooks no contradiction, compliance; that
was what they; and you; you.
and you too, you ~~the happiest cynics I know~~
I know, while ~~I'm the saddest optimist~~

FRIENDS

friends
of
my
mother's
used
to
call
me
small
change. i
had no
idea
how short
i was.

FRIENDS

Friends
of
my
mother's
used
to
call
me
small
change. i
had no
idea
how short
i was.

MORNING

In music
my favorite instruments
are violin-cello,
oboe and upright
bass. I let
myself in key
though it's the
flute that has me
humming with
my banjo; strings
and twenty reeds, some
voice to pierce
the gloom, the
plunking vibraphone
the flute, the
cornet, the
bone, thirds
[illegible] or Beiderbecke,
trumpet with
the bass, the drum-
mer the [illegible]
sounds right. I
wake up to this rhythm-
most mornings
some penny-
whistle, some gong,
castanets, How can I
[illegible] [illegible].

MORNING

In music
my favorite instruments
are violin—cello
oboe and upright
bass. I let
myself in key
though it's the
flute that has me
humming with
my banjo; strings
and throaty reeds, some
voice to pierce
the gloom, the
[-----] vibraphone
the flute, the
cornet the
bone. If
Clifford or Beiderbeck
bumped with
the bass, the [----]—
hum the djuku
sounds right. I
wake up to this rhythm—
most mornings
Some penny-
whistle, some gong,
castanets, How can't I
have shamal

CRITIQUE

I draw badly
Well; neighbor's
Noses, frowns, lips,
Eyes, shoulders
Much too
Narrow for
The chest on
Breasts & bellies. Hands
Are what
Draw me
Into arms, knuckles
& joints of
All kinds. I get a blade
Here – a bone
There. A flight
Of birds headed south
To somewhere
Take a leg,
A tent, a
Bike leaned
Against a magnolia.
Garbage. If
Grants were given out
For that I'd be as rich as
David Hammons,
Maybe. I'd get a car, paper,
[illegible] Show.
[illegible].

11/28/15

CRITIQUE

I draw badly
well; neighbor's
noses, frowns lips,
eyes, shoulders
much too
narrow for
the chest on
Breasts & bellies, hands
are what
Drew me
Into this. Knuckles
& joints of
all kinds. I get a blade
Here—a bone
There. A flight
Of birds headed south
To somewhere
Take a leg,
A head, a
Bike leaned
Against a magnolia.
Garbage. If
grunts were given out
for that I'd be as rich as
David Hammons,
Maybe. I'd get a car, paper,
chow.

11/28/15

Everything
is about posture
Or a fine
Definition of the
Lack of it. Humans
Tend not to only
If they are serious These
have an angle.

GRACE

What she taught you
holding you back from yourself
as you took three uncertain

steps toward the corner
was if you fell
you picked yourself up

or shit if you went too fast
would have to learn
to keep up

with yourself, and later, dragging
you behind her through
the shops along Bathgate

from which the emanating
smells of garlic and rye bread
exciting your nostrils

mingled with the sight
of wrinkled sausages, coupons hung
from hooks upside down

in the windows oranges & onions acutely
marrying the sense, learned you
took a number, waited

for your turn because
that was your number; no stepping
out of line with her

you kept one hand open in your lap
at the table, mumbled grace so the Lord would know
mumbling made us more than merely
something to eat. (some ~~place)~~ means, some place.)

GRACE

My Dad
1920
1984

What she taught you
holding you back from yourself
as you took three uncertain

steps toward the corner
was if you fell
you picked yourself up

or that if you went too fast
~~you~~ would have to learn
to keep up

with yourself, and later, dragging
you behind her through
the shops along Bathgate

from which the emanating
smells of garlic and rye bread
exciting your nostrils

mingled with the sight
of wrinkled sausages, capons hung
from hooks upside down

in the windows' vicinity – oranges & onions

marrying the senses, learned you
took a number, waited

for your turn because
that was your number: no stepping
out of line with her.

You kept one hand ~~in~~ open in your lap
at the table, mumbled grace ~~because~~ ~~so~~ so the ~~[illegible]~~ lord would know ~~[illegible]~~
~~[illegible]~~.
mumbling made us more than merely
~~[illegible]~~ something to eat. (some ~~place~~ meant, some place.)

CG: You know, like a guy named Ed Kelly, a piano player, Donald Baily--a drummer that used to play with Jimmy Smith, Pharaoh Saunders was out there--Eddie Henderson was there, and so I just put my horn out and I started to play in local places because I didn't know what to do! I didn't know how to make a living playing music. I was sitting in at a jam session and Pharaoh Saunders walks in. We were playing "Polkadots and Moonbeams, I'll never forget that, and I played a duet with Pharaoh and Eddie Henderson showed up. That's how I met Eddie. Yoshie's was the name of the place.

JF: Yoshie's?

CG: Yeah. In Berkeley. And then I started playing at Milestones out there in San Francisco. Sonny Buxton, that was his club. I was in the house band. You know, I just listened to different musicians, Gaylord Birch, Waheem Young, lotta good guys, man--so three years later a friend says, Look, you gotta go to New York, the stuff you wanna do. That ain't happenin' anywhere else but New York, you gotta go there because that's where all the cats are. So he encouraged me to leave.

JF: And what was your experience when you got to New York?

CG: I was just trying to play, man. As soon as I got here I want to the Blue Note and just sat in--you know, a jam session--I went up to Harlem, I went out to Queens--to the Village Door in Queens, went to Carmichaels, I hooked up with Wig Flight--you know, whose a tenor player, and he kind of showed me the ropes about Harlem and Brooklyn--the Valhal, that was one of the first places that I played, over there on Fulton Street in downtown Brooklyn--

JF: And so you've been working with various big bands--

CG: Yeah,

JF: You've been working with the Mingus big band?

CG: Yeah the first big band I was working with was Charlie Persip's big band. I used to write some stuff for him. And them I went out with Lionel Hampton; I was with the Ellington Orchestra, Mercer Ellington conducting, and then I worked with Maria Schnieder, the Vanguard Orchestra--pretty much every big band in NY.

JF: The Basic Band?

CG: Yeah--Frank Foster conducting. That was about 1995.

JF: And how did you come into contact with nublu--and the bands you play with at nublu--what bands do you play with at nublu?

MORPH

Willow and larch
Give way to scrub, scotch
Pine. Baltimore oriole
To NY sand crane: Avoid
Long Island Expressway,
Route Meadowbrook
Through dunes.
Fly over creek
And estuary, loop under
High stone
Relief of obelisk stabbing nude
Blue sky, skirt
Sea of umbrellas
Reaching the breakers. skip, sail
Over the cyclopean orb
Of lighthouse—denizens pejoratively
Beautiful, ship-shape
The pejorative women peripatetic or
Supine as bronze
Odalisks, thonged
As lutes, violins, guitars; and out
There, blue,
Formerly plenipotent in what had been his own
World-Leviathan cruising; Leviathan, poor
Briny Leviathan.

MY WORD

I give my word
freely: it doesn't cost much
for me to keep plus
it's no fun. Imagine
a word kept quiet.
If I had one it would mean plenty
less than George, by George George—
George, did you get that?
How is that for inspiration,
a fine lyric, a rhyme,
what does it mean from charted
if not the same thing?
Shoes are shoes. Hawkins need
jerking otherwise
what's the point. I'm afraid
there's where it's like
new music. It's like
when your lover has
not gone. It's like not entertaining
the babies. It's like me
inventing blues.

and swinging it.

MY WORD

I give my word
freely: it doesn't cost much
for me to keep plus
its no fun. Imagine
a word kept quiet.
If I had one it would mean plenty
less than George, by George George—
George, did you get that?
How is that for inspiration,
a fine lyric, a rhyme
What does it mean translated
if not the same thing?
Shoes are shoes. Hank's neck
turning, otherwise
what's the point. I'm afraid
there is [----]. It's like
new music. It's like
when your lover has
not gone. It's like not entertaining
the basics. It's like me
inventing blue.
and swinging it.

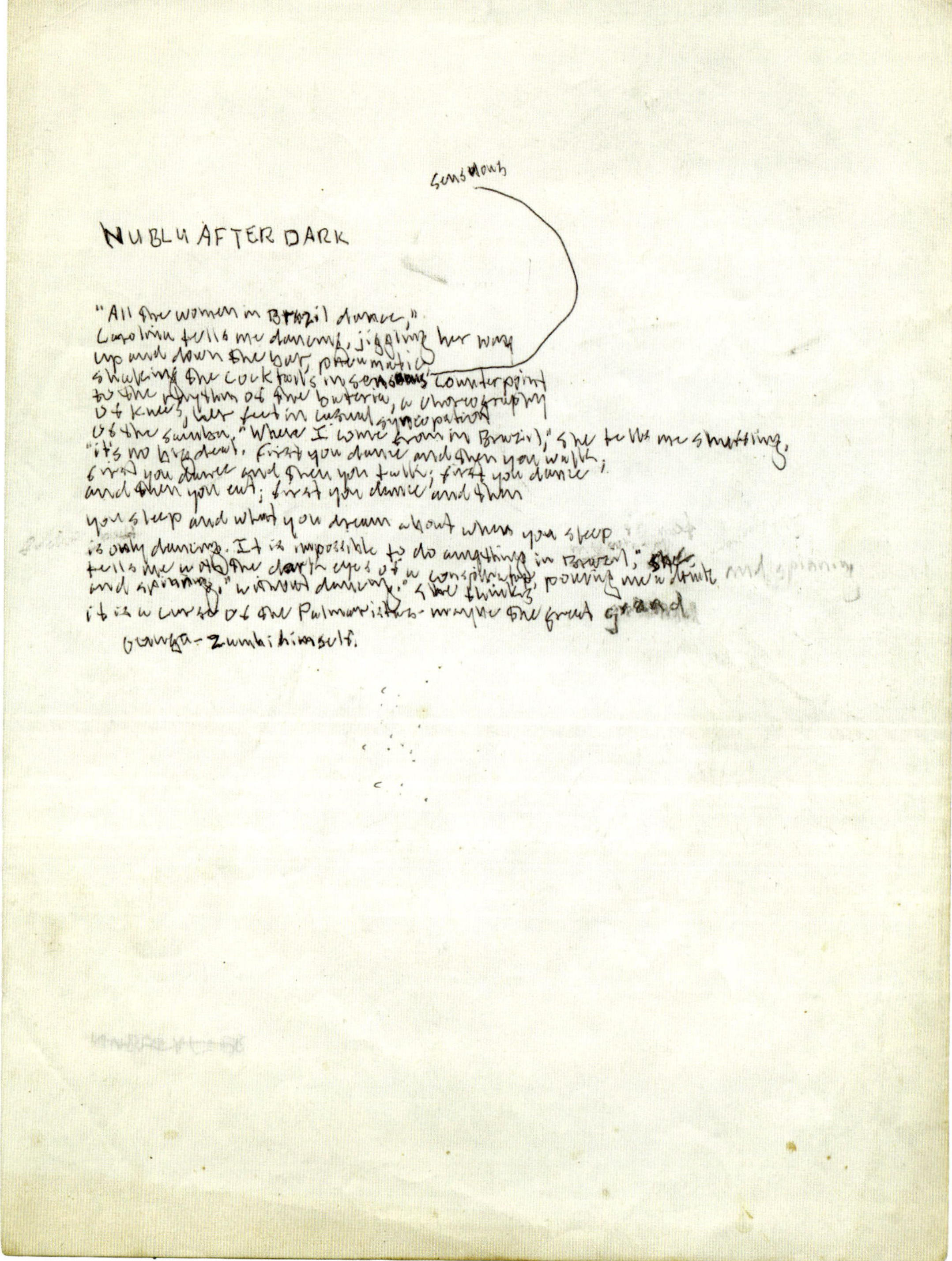

sensuous

NUBLU AFTER DARK

"All the women in Brazil dance,"
Carolina tells me dancing, jiggling her way
up and down the bar, pneumatic
shaking the cocktails in sensuous counterpoint
to the rhythm of the bateria, a choreography
of knees, her feet in casual syncopation
of the samba. "Where I come from in Brazil," she tells me shuffling,
"it's no big deal. First you dance and then you walk,
first you dance and then you talk; first you dance
and then you eat; first you dance and then
you sleep and what you dream about when you sleep
is only dancing. It is impossible to do anything in Brazil," she
tells me with the dark eyes of a conspirator, pouring me a drink and spinning
and spinning, "without dancing." She thinks
it is a curse of the Palmaristas—maybe the great grand
Ganga-Zumbi himself.

NUBLU AFTER DARK

"All the women in Brazil dance,"
Carolina tells me dancing, jiggling her way
up and down the bar, pneumatic,
shaking the cocktails, in sensuous counterpoint
to the rhythm of the bateria, a choreography
of knees, her feet in casual syncopation
of the samba. "Where I come from in Brazil," she tells me, shouting,
"it's no big deal. First you dancc and then you walk,
first you dance and then you talk; first you dance
and then you eat; first you dance and then
you sleep and what you dream about when you sleep
is only dancing. It is impossible to do anything in Brazil," she
tells me with the dark eyes of a conspiracy, pouring me a drink
it is a curse of the Palmaristas—maybe the great grand
Ganga-Zumbi himself.

ONE NIGHT

One night
I dropped my
eraser down
the toilet.
Shit I said,
shit. A
friend said
that's what I produce
anyway. All
my friends, all my relatives
are so doggone
predictable no
matter who
or what I have here (talk
about your pipes, your misfits), everything I own
            out of sight even
with my
constitution
            Talk about in-
spiring! Talk about
            your culture,
(your caste).

ONE NIGHT

One night
I dropped my
eraser down
the toilet bowl
Shit I said,
shit ... A
friend said
that's what I produce
anyway. All
my friends, all my relatives
are so doggone
predictable no
matter who
or what I have here, (talk
about your
pipes, your misfits), everything I own
out of sight even
with my
constitution. Talk
about in-
spiring! Talk about
your culture,
your
(....) caste

culture, your ...
class ...
...
stick of something
sk...
or something.

RECYCLE
PLEASE
recycleplease.org

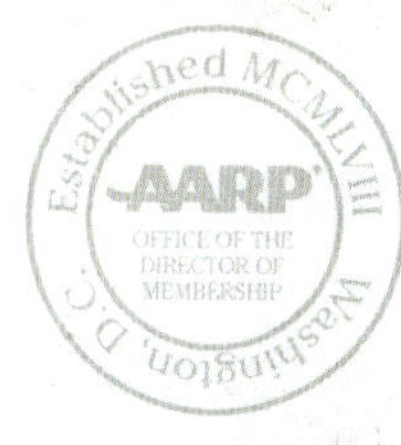

Dear Mr. Farris,

Please keep this card until you receive your Membership Kit. It will include your new card, as well as complete details on how to take advantage of your member benefits.

I'm sure you'll find that using just a few of your benefits can more than repay the cost of your membership.

You'll also appreciate AARP's trustworthy information and resources. It can help you protect your health, your money and your career, and make the most of life over 50.

Welcome to AARP!

Sincerely,

Steve Cone
Director of Membership

P.S. Return the form above with your payment to receive your Mini Day Bag — **FREE.** Your membership is guaranteed if you're 50 or over, whether working or retired.

WHAT YOU GET	PRICE
✓ 12 month membership in AARP	$16
✓ 12 month membership for your spouse or partner	*Included*
✓ Award-winning *AARP The Magazine* that will help you feel great, save money and have fun.	*Included*
✓ Access to exclusive products: health insurance, dental coverage, eye care, pharmacy.	*Included*
✓ 10 issues of The *AARP Bulletin* Newspaper	*Included*
✓ Access to discounts on hotels, car rentals, cruises, home security, cell phone service, and more.	*Included*
✓ Representation in Washington and all 50 states. Fighting age discrimination, protecting pension rights, Social Security, Medicare.	*Included*

ONLY $16

As an AARP member you know that you're supporting the nation's largest non-profit organization that fights for the rights of all people over 50. Whether you're retired or working, you can make a difference and we invite you to join us today.

DRAWING

I draw like a precocious
ten-year old. I draw blanks and make vivid color
in black graphite, use self-portraits to suggest
blue, anger say, to suggest red. If I
am brown, it is only in the context
of the context, a wink to suggest the bright, the clever.
I make a case for green in spring of a black leaf
on a tree that is entirely blank—
except for in a couple of places and perhaps
for how big it is (never never more
than a solid inch or two). Just talk
about space, some cloud, and
boy, just try to let
a cat get into
there, a car, a presumptuous flight
of birds. I've got to be
so careful about
careful about the [illegible] bone in my
[illegible]
nose. [illegible]
[illegible] once, [illegible]
[illegible]
[illegible] I am the
c[illegible]
a[illegible] get paid [illegible] to be!
[illegible]
is music. At least. Now [illegible]

DRAWING

I draw
like a precocious
10 year old: I draw blanks
and make vivid color
in black graphite, use self-portraits
to suggest blue, anger say,
to suggest red. If I am
brown, it is
only in the context
of the context, a wink
to suggest the bright, the clever. I
make
a case for green in spring of a black leaf
on a tree that
is entirely black
except for in
a couple of places and perhaps
how big it is (never
never more than a solid inch
[illegible]
two). Just talk
about space, some cloud, and O boy just try
to let a cat get onto
there, a car, a flight of
birds. I've
got to be O so
careful about the
goddamn bone in my nose.

[illegible] goddamn bone.

Angle. You are
always after
some angle... ~~[illegible]~~ ol'
angle: talk about a breast-
you could ever have
it straight

Angle. You are
always after
some angle… same ol'
angle; talk about a blast—
you can't even have
it straight

5

on a long long long long long long long long long long long long long
roll & dat tobbaco
wanna you you you
corn ball, dat bullshit period shit a big pool, baby, it might be
Tutu too long dat. Cow, hey whence
was I me me me I want

to up I want to be what I wanna seem
cool cow / you you want you gittin' quite outa'

in dat gol' darn basement, in dat hay hay hay hay hay,
hand-down dere

La Mama
47 GT JONES ST
3. PM

CLUE
(found poem)?

One of these ~~autumn~~ mornings
~~I'll ... ~~
I'm going to find myself ~~...~~ old 5:14
out of here, ~~...~~
~~becoming an~~ old
a monster like ~~...~~

or Kim Fu... simply
reason to things. I imagine
that. Seeing things
the way they should be should not appear
be, the said ... and those you ...
~~the wrong word~~ turning
~~back towards~~ what
makes what some truth is
must be some ... revolution
some clear light driving
nothing in the road ...
no blind colours
...
~~no~~ dip for the bread. It
could be
"good", it could be ~~...~~ bad, some future bend
for it, crying, "WRY!"
Others wail, "FRUIT!"

John ...
(347) 344-5446
Cust. Svc. (800) 365-9044
Con. # 3111306

NO JOKE

dragging myself
through 3rd street
& across avenues
depends on the kindness
of strangers, cars, trucks, bicycles
refuse to run me over. The other
day a bus stopped just short
of a crutch at a curb I was
hanging precariously from
& swung out to miss me. it was
an old man who
was getting on that alerted
the driver & a young hoodie
that grabbed my pack: i
thought he was going to run, but he didn't.
"Watch out pop!" he said, solicitously, &
never asked me for
a quarter. Maybe more
people should be crippled: even cops.

All my
models
appear
to have
great ~~gobs~~ of snot
~~strands~~
hanging
from their
nostrils
or to
have read
David
James on
wall.

I just
~~come~~ to
find most
of them
to be
somewhat
aloof,
you know,
snotty.

All my
models
appear
to have
great gobs
of snot
hanging
from their
nostrils
or to
have read
Darius
James on
Walt.
I just
come to
find most
of them
to be
somewhat
aloof,
you know,
snotty.

QUITE

Magnificent character—grand, hot,
Are adjectives I term the work when I manage
To manage it to my satisfaction, same

Intent in the neck & shoulders
If not the face. The externalized should be clearly
Internal gazing wherever for what while still,

Can almost beg attention, a smoking
worker. That's class I say, that's culture, proud
Or not. It's not Paris or Memphis or not.

The Khan's music should be clear
Even if he is not carrying an instrument one can
See, perhaps the importance of the

Throat even hidden, kept warm
From view. I say I am getting good at this lying
The world calls art, or not on the way,

The vocabulary missing, sadly, sadly,
Added to a pile of do. That's doing, right, I say,
or not, that's doing;

Get the kid, get the carriage, a poem.
No one can teach you this unless it is an architect
Of some pile [illegible], disorganized;

Moving.

QUITE

Magnificent characters, grand, hot,
Are adjectives I term the work when I manage
To manage it to my satisfaction, same

Intent in the neck & shoulders
If not the face. The externalized should be clearly
Internal gazing wherever for what while still,

Can almost beg attention, a smoking
worker. That's class I say, that's culture, proud
or not. It's not Paris or Memphis or not.
The Khan's music should be clear
Even if he is not carrying an instrument one can
see, perhaps the importance of the

Throat even hidden, kept warm
From view. I say I am getting good at this lying
The world calls art, or not on its way,

The vocabulary missing, sadly, sadly,
Added to a pile of do. That's doing, right, I say,
doing right or not, that's doing,

Get the kid, get the carriage, a poem.
No one can teach you this unless it is an architect
of some pile featureless, disorganized,
            moving.

MINI-DRAMA

Time: The present.
Place: A metropolis

Two gentlemen standing on a corner. One of them has lost his sight.
UNSIGHTED: (feeling) Ish-Ish-ah's fum N'Awlins. Red Light.
An tries ta look onna bright side. Dem goddamned glasses was
'spensive! Cain't eben use 'em no mo.

MINI-DRAMA

Time: The present
Place: A metropolis

Two gentleman standing on a corner. One of them has lost his sight
UNSIGHTED: (feeling) Ish-Ish-ah's fum N'Awlins. Red Light.
Ah tried ta look onna bright side. Dem goddamned glasses was 'spensive! Cain't cben use 'em nomo.

CLUE

The
other
day
I made
a drawing
of butch morris.
I showed it to
a friend who
said it was alright.
i just couldn't go
to the bank
with it. hey,
that's what friends
are for.
class. &
stuff. (drawing you here
is a sketchy situation
at best.)

LORE

Kensington Horror abuts El Reverendo
Pedro Pietri's way: the lord of Kensington Horror
sits high in a [illegible] on his castle
[illegible] excrement for who: "a
little piss makes green," he says. "I only like
the good shit, [illegible]
I listen to Miles Davis, Shirley Scott, Gilly Coffins, and Frank.
Looking out that window,"
he says pointing to where the
El Reverendo
singing Pedro Pietri's way is characterizing me,
makes me see red and more red. [illegible] too much. I'd put that guy
behind the eight ball if I could, but he's dead.
"My hair is white. Around here," he says, / the purple apoplectic,
"I'm an institution! Get me?" when it comes to whirling squares
and Fibonacci, I'm Monet, — I'm Monet!"

I'm [illegible] [illegible]
is sharp as autumn.

LORE

Kenkeleba House abuts El Reverendo
Pedro Pietri Way: the bard of Kenkeleba House
sits high in a turret in his castle
mixing excrement for what: "a
little piss makes green," he says, "I only like
the good shit, for the blues
I listen to Miles Davis, Shirley Scott, Gilly Coggins, and Frank.
Looking out that window.
He says pointing to where the
El Reverendo [---] Pedro Pietri Way is changing me
makes me see red, and more red, it's too much. I'd put that song
behind the eight ball if I could, but he's dead.
"My hair is white. Around here," he says. /the purple plainly apoplectic
"I'm the institution. Get me?" When it comes to whirling squares
and Fibonacci, I'm Monet,—I'm Monet!"

POEM

the
only
sin
was
that
we
did
not
do
it.

i
keep
missing
stuff.

it
must
be
my
phone.

POEM

the
only
sin
was
that
we
did
not
do
it.
i
keep
missing
stuff.
it
must
be
my
phone.

NUMBER

If it's the blues
or oddmeters
that wake me
~~[illegible]~~.

Going down-
stairs running my mouth
wishing neighbors good
morning
on passing, puffing
like a madman.
Now that's class where I
come from.

You call it
music; you say,
"That's not
music"; you invented
it, class.

There
is a bell, loose-
ly, ~~[illegible]~~ loosely (the longest
~~[illegible]~~. John from Mississippi. Spell
that: M-I-
SS-
IPP
I, some drum, (~~[illegible]~~ parenthetically
that's e-vil; you some
girl
crossing, on line,
shakin'
~~[illegible]~~ Elvis flashing a
Hawk, go
~~[illegible]~~
outside, try some number!
Talk about ~~[illegible]~~
romance) dressed now for atmosphere.
~~[illegible]~~! some
swazi, some
Yoruba when I get back, the banjo
~~[illegible]~~ old
~~[illegible]~~ the wedding, ~~[illegible]~~
some oud, some
haze, shout, Hey!
You gave me, kid, banana bread / and coffee ~~[illegible]~~

TALK

Talk
About poem,
The paper –
I'm writing
IS indecent,
Eye–
Eye–
eye–
eye– cont
see– gimme

Some
Glasses so eye–eye so eye
can see what's
In 'im pleas

I–eye

stand
In around
A bit– bid– bit at
A– A– A–
Crown– get– gip me some
trumpets
then
We talk about the
[illegible],

MUSE

What I love
is a blind man
telling me
I can't draw.
I tell him
he can't feel
the ass. I
tell him go
on, try
just for once (for what it's worth
to feel its
canvas, to [illegible]
[illegible],
might see
something outside
something besides
that hyperbole
get himself a grip
a real guitar and
sing so [illegible]. [illegible]
that's class, that's
[illegible] on. [illegible]
his own

VANPAGE
05-115 89
-2880

MUSE

What I love
is a blind man
telling me
I can't draw.
I tell him
he can't feel
the ass. I
tell him go
on try
just for once (for what's worth
to feel
curves, to
let it in. He
might see
something outside
something besides
that hyperbole
get himself a grip
and a real guitar and
song, go forth. NOW
that's class, that's
hands on.

I HAVE

I have
some great drawings
That I did
when I waz
About seven years old mentally.

A friend said they were "cute". Anyway
I still have them. Nowadays I'm
Actually learning to make a penny!
At last,
Fine art. Bas relief. Semi-
Literacy.

I HAVE

I have
Some great drawings
That I did
When I was
About seven years old mentally.

A friend said they were "cute". Anyway
I still have that. Nowadays I'm
Actually learning to make a penny!
At last,
Fine art. Bas Relief semi-
literary.

AFBLICK

3

3

I might hi
gi it tu
maggie! that
ain no
fiction – that's
pretty sevith.

I might e²ⁿ

Gi'you girl
I don't
TRUE. Dash
for true!
on time! period –
ah don't

no where ya git
"it" from, period. poetry –
yo' hand in dash. period. Dash –
dat on time –
dey got what you like, comma,
period. punctuation comma
all on time – dash – right
on time – dash, comma left
on line, you
period comma, period
you got right on
time yo dash: now yo hand
in it.
Time comma period – now
dat's for true poetry –
poetry right on time coma poetry period period.
Now dat's english, you hear dat question
marks with a capital and a p. full stop, period!

over, comma, dash, now they go
git yo' ass,
period. Ah cain', crazy
Baby!! Oh, my love!!! you mind yo'
bidness an let dem min' dem bidness
& you let dem min'
deres. & ain' dat
a fawn coma commin ain'
dat a bitch. Dat's why
dey come now wid all
dis poetry, dis
comma, period. Fug fug fug
I guess oughtta put you on da fagah all
space dis
poetry, dash, coma comma
period!!
Hysterical. Now
dat's english wid a
small capital: now
dat's a fawn coma comma period. Ma
mama cum git me — gi'
dem a chance. (period.) see? Dat's why
dey go on wid dat shit shit —
takes up a lotta space, hey? Some
square
take up a lotta space period. They
couldn' learn from
me, period. Dey just
didn wanna, hey. You just cain spell
cain, wanna spell? on da L train?
LEAH Heah? Now
Let you — put a spell on dat! Jesus! Cross! I

guess Ah ain' gonna live, Icey. Money!! wee, dat [illegible] & dat didah - dey dah
Fuck'em, period.

SOPHIST

My work
is seen
to best
advantage
viewed
in the
dark. That way
the lines are
lost
in reality
talk about missing teeth
the abstraction talk
about a blast! Same
new moon.

SOPHIST

My work
is seen
to best
advantage
viewed
in the
dark. That way
the lines are
frankly lost
in reality.
talk about missing teeth
the abstraction. Talk
about a blast! Same
new moon.

II

People think
I sit here
and do
nothing. ~~and~~
I dream. I
dream
the Rabbit, I
do
Billie, maybe
Mahalia.
That's gospel. If
I weren't
so bad with names
there would be
others. Plenty
of them. People tell me
that's a lot
of jazz. I have
gas. When it
comes to ~~[illegible]~~ that stuff
I belch in tune or worse. I
veritably light up the joint.
That's something.

TEACHING Pt. II

People think
I sit here
and do
nothing.
I [---]. I
do
the Rabbit, I
do
Billie, maybe
Mahalia.
That's gospel. If
I weren't
so bad with names
there would be
others. Plenty
of them. People tell me
that's a lot
of jazz. I have
gas. When it
comes to that stuff
I belch in tune or worse! I
veritably light up the joint.
That's something.

VANESSA

your ego
is in love
with you:
it always
loves to
see you
coming, sex
appeal &
all, the
lines of
hair over
your own
shoulders,
a small
cascade
down your
own back
you always
~~[illegible]~~
your own back.
[illegible]
shoulder ~~to a~~ shoulder,
shoulders, [illegible]
[illegible] things. [illegible]
[illegible]
[illegible]

VAINESSA

Your ego
is in love
with you:
it always
loves to
see you
coming. sex
appeal &
all the
lines of
hair over
your own
shoulder,
a small
cursive
down your
own back
you always
manage
your own back.

shoulder-to-
shoulder, conspirators.

10

"With the white man even the weather is predictable. He is
on his way to Mars. That's what the slaves called him when they learned
his language. Mars. What kin I say 'bout dat?" said Ricky. "The needy mutts, he took mine. Corn. Yams. The only thing they can't
do, they say, is trust a nigger to get it right unless it's wrong every
goddamn time, and you can bet on that! That's why I joined the
church—'cause I am not a betting man.

I want to understand what is known, and to discover
what is unknown.

~~[illegible]~~ Count Money, he was Count II.

She responded to me
with, "yes—I
do have remarkable hands,
don't I." Lay
to say the least

If life doesn't do much else,
it will kill you.

Vanessa
347
210 ~~[illegible]~~59

55 and
Myisha
1877-2165166
X4298

IDT Energy
Ratoshin
(855)283-9239

"With the white man even the weather is predictable. He is on his way to Mars. That's what the slaves called him when they learned his language. Mars. He needed nuts, he took mine or yours. What kin I say 'bout that," said Ricky. The only thing they can't do, they say, is trust a nigger to git it right unless it's wrong every goddamn time, and you bet on that! That's why I joined the church—'cause I am not a bettin' man.

I want to understand what is known, and to discover what is unknown.

Count Money, he was Count II.

She responded to me
with "yes—I
do have remarkable hands,
don't I." Love
to say the least

If life doesn't do much else,
it will kill you.

14

SCUTTLEBUTT

"If God had given camels wings, those jockeys would really have dropped some shit on us"

"The president was really nice to have visited us, and to have given the city 20 whole billion dollars, America."

"Members of the Board of Elections were told to leave so that some votes might have gotten lost."

"Behind the barriers the mayor appears perennial, like Fiorello.

"Kabul is so used to bombs, over there they call them rain."

"Soldiers invading Afghanistan tend to become heroin addicts.

"There is a strong relationship between Morphine and the Khyber Pass.

"If you're not with us, you're against us. That's because of our pluralistic form of government."

"The Attorney General sounds like John Wayne."

"Bring back Elian Gonzales."

"Baseball was returned to the free world."

"~~John Wayne is a good person~~ [illegible] ~~the man is Forks'~~ [illegible]

~~[illegible]~~

"~~[illegible] dogs out~~!"

SCUTTLEBUTT

"If God had given camels wings, those jockeys would
really have dropped some shit on us"

"The president was really nice to have visited, and to have given
the city 20 whole billion dollars, American."

"Members of the Board of Elections were told to have so [---]
some votes might have gotten lost."

"Behind the barriers the mayor appears perennial, like Fiorello."

"Kabul is so used to bombs, over there they call them rain."

"Soldiers invading Afghanistan tend to become heroin addicts."

"There is a strong relationship between morphine and the Khyber Pass."

"If you're not with us, you're against us. That's because of our pluralistic form
of government."

"The Attorney General sounds like John Wayne."

"Bring back Elian Gonzales."

"Baseball has returned to the free world."

You knit sweaters, I knit
brows, usually
my own. You wear
scarves, I wear
frowns.
You find that ironic this or
or that a sneer.

YOU KNIT SWEATERS

You knit sweaters, I knit
brows, usually
my own. You wear
scarves, I wear
frowns.
You find that ironic this
or that a sneer.

YOU SAY

friend, you say
it wasn't
said [illegible] I
I couldn't draw
what was said
you said by way of example
was at my age
my ability
was limited strictly
to the [illegible]: &
when it came
to lines, in
place of shadow
what you saw
[illegible] place of mine at best
[illegible] was the
universal dark, a mere suggestion; subjects
[illegible], objects
sketched; a — thrown up, thrown out,
hand, an eye,
that old hat,
maybe me. It wasn't that it was not
[illegible] the
problem was
my [illegible] at [illegible]
was [illegible] struggle, [illegible].

I say, see,
that's just
like [illegible]; you say "Hey that's funny." (I say that's good
I'm not even trying
to be funny)
[illegible] I'm not even trying to
be funny but [illegible] if it makes you
laugh. That's something. When it
comes [illegible] and my bad line.
[illegible]. How about that.

YOU SAY

friend, you say
it wasn't
said I
I couldn't draw—
what was said
you said by way of example
was at my age
my ability
was limited strictly

to the elementary: &
when it came
to lines; in
place of shadow
what you saw
at best
was the
universal dark & mere suggestion; subjects
objects
sketched; a
hand thrown up, thrown out, an eye
that old hat—
maybe me. It wasn't that it was not
allowed the
problem was
my sense of being
was clearly struggle, while

I say, see
that's just
like old me—bland: you say "Hey that's funny."
I say that's good I'm not even trying to
be funny but darling if it makes you
laugh that's something. When it
comes to trouble and my bloodline.
How about that.

That's why
they wanted you old
boy, didn't you, boy
spoiling chasing thing,
spoiling
plays, you were there!

You
always
wore a
tie &
loved poetry
women & scotch &
a good beer
the thing about you
was thought you always
thought they loved you,
the thing was
you thought a
lot & they
kept you
laughing
at old bars you
wish for
a lot of these things
but you
only got a lot
of a few: maybe
in your old
town you thought a lot
you thought that that should
take you somewhere,
you thought how was that
for losing the blues you thought
hey,
about
a good club, somewhere, you
thought that was
class, didn't you somewhere / first, first month!

Backwoods
boy

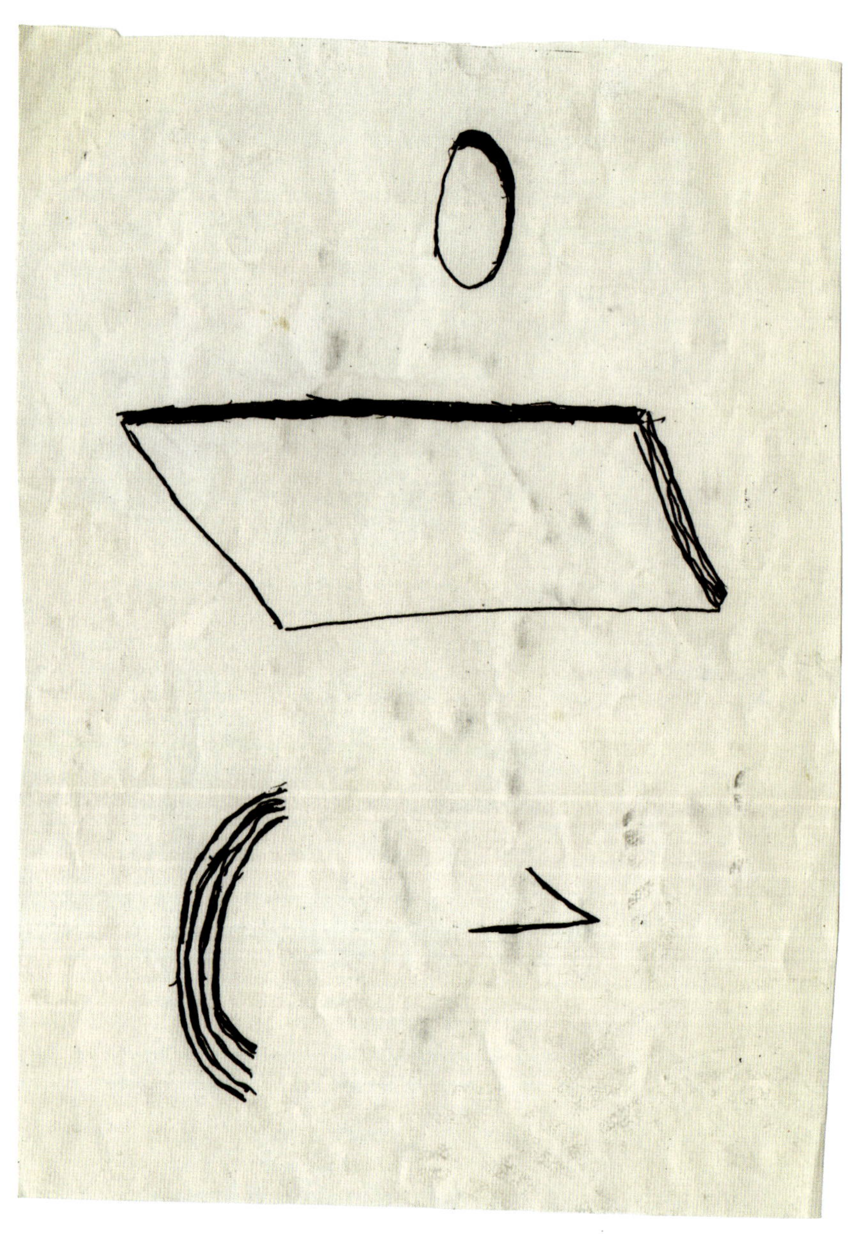

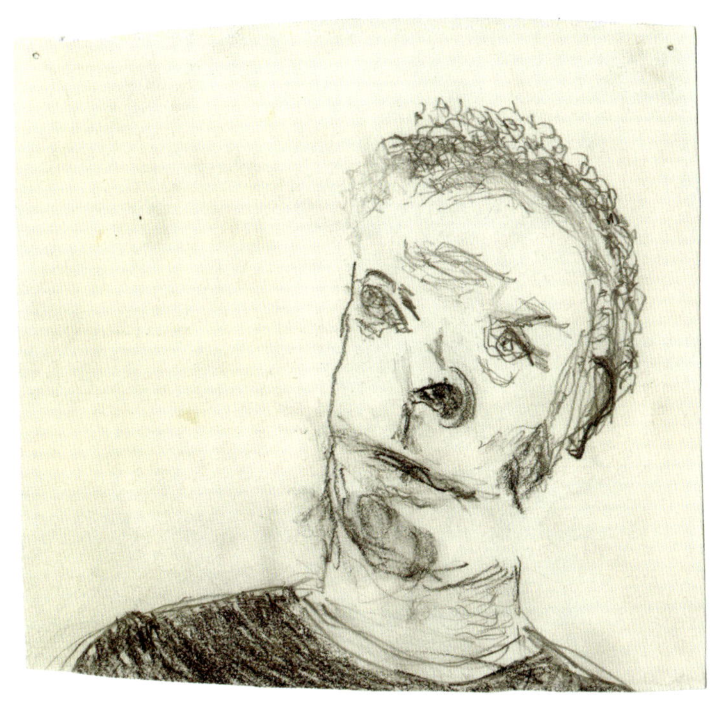

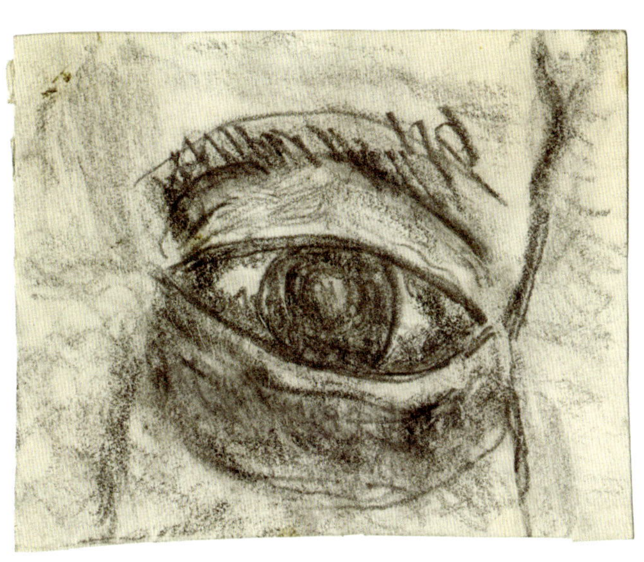

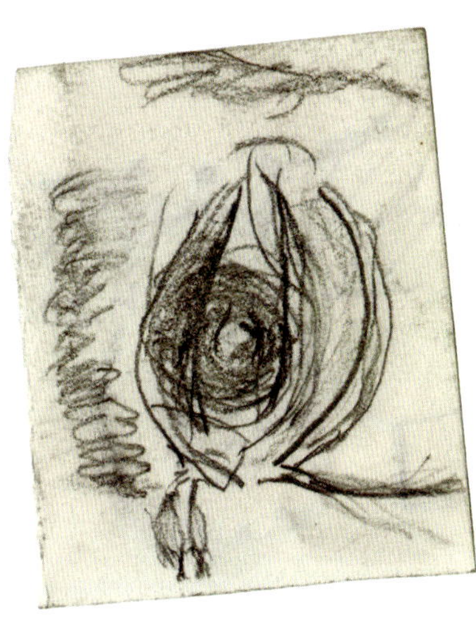

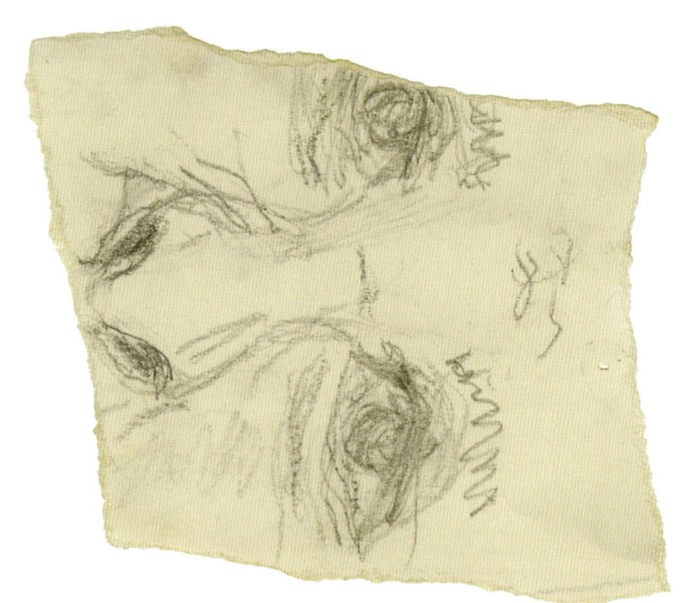

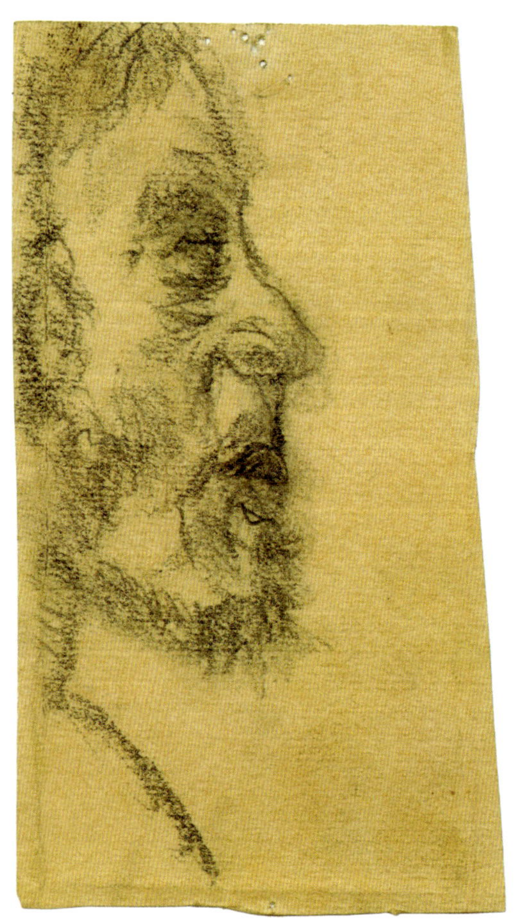

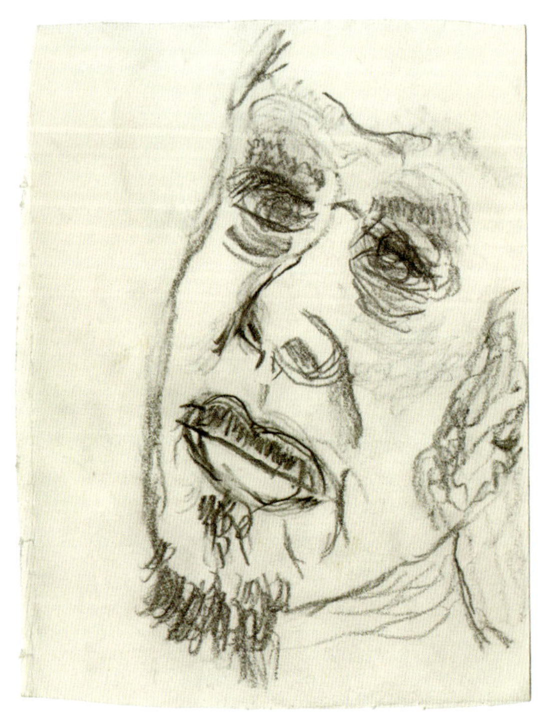

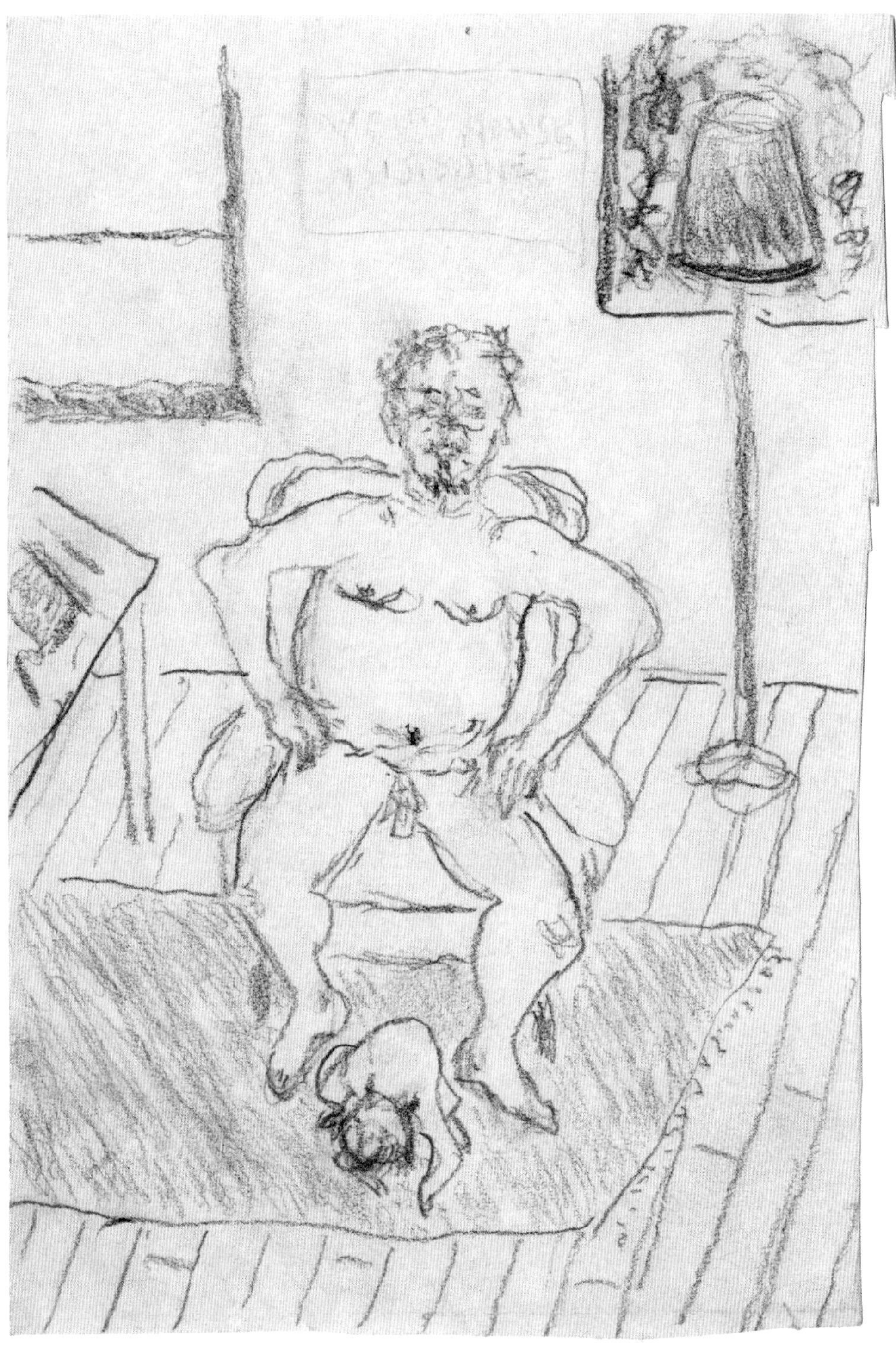

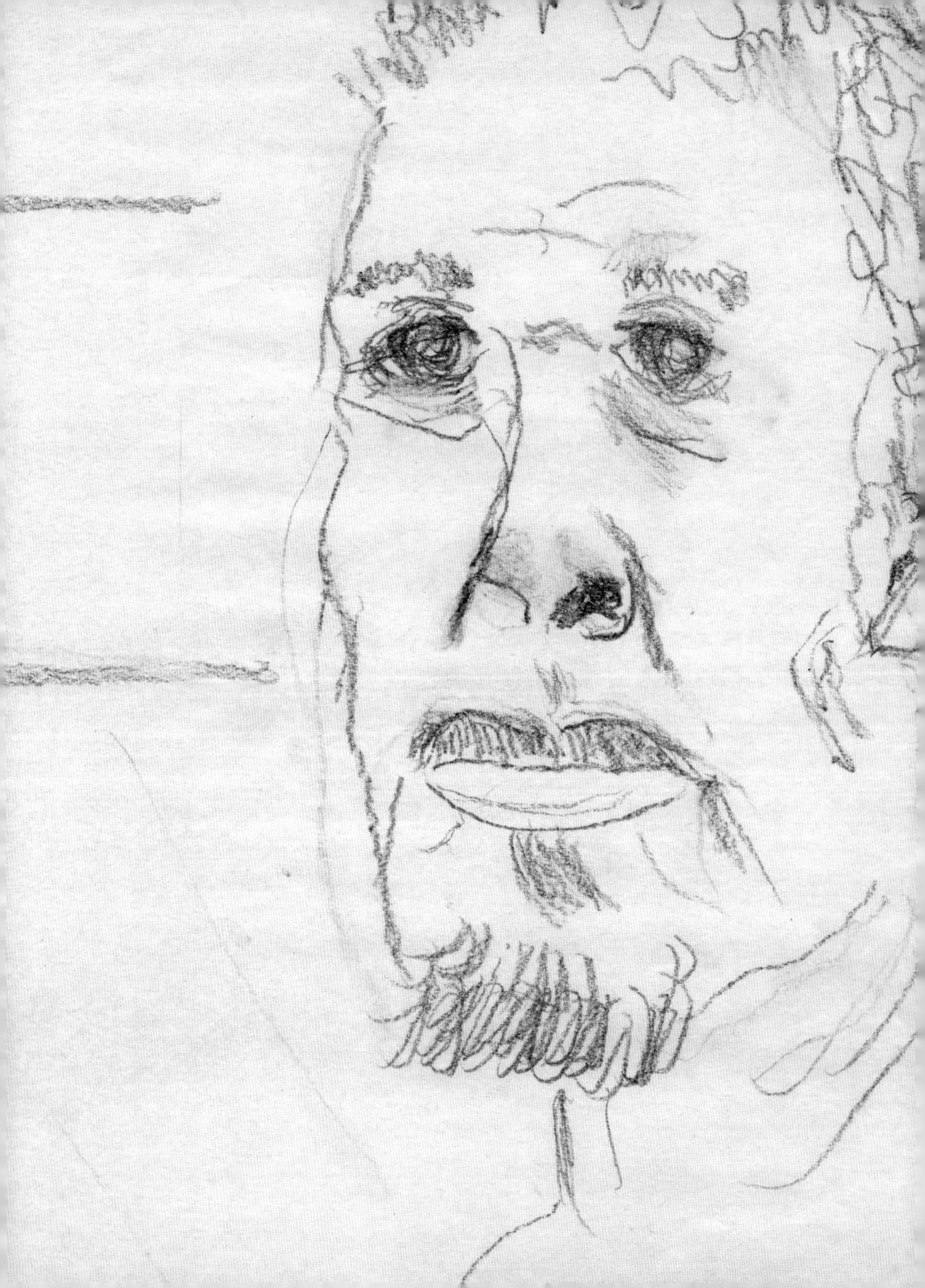

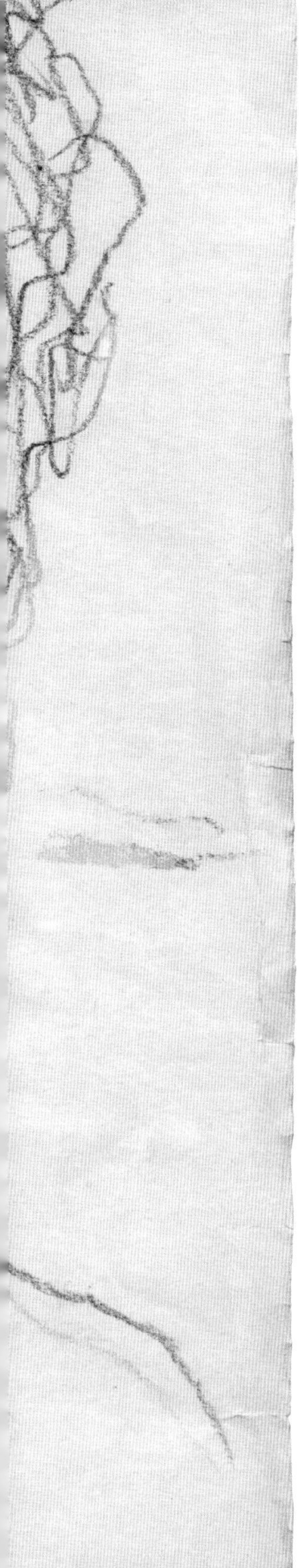

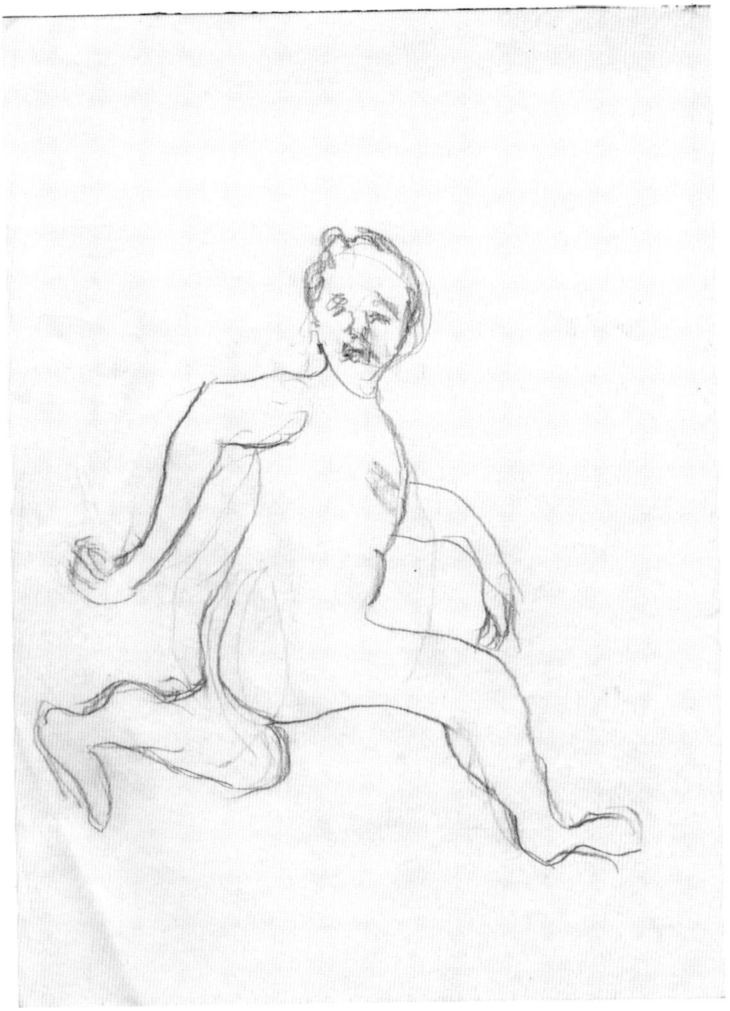

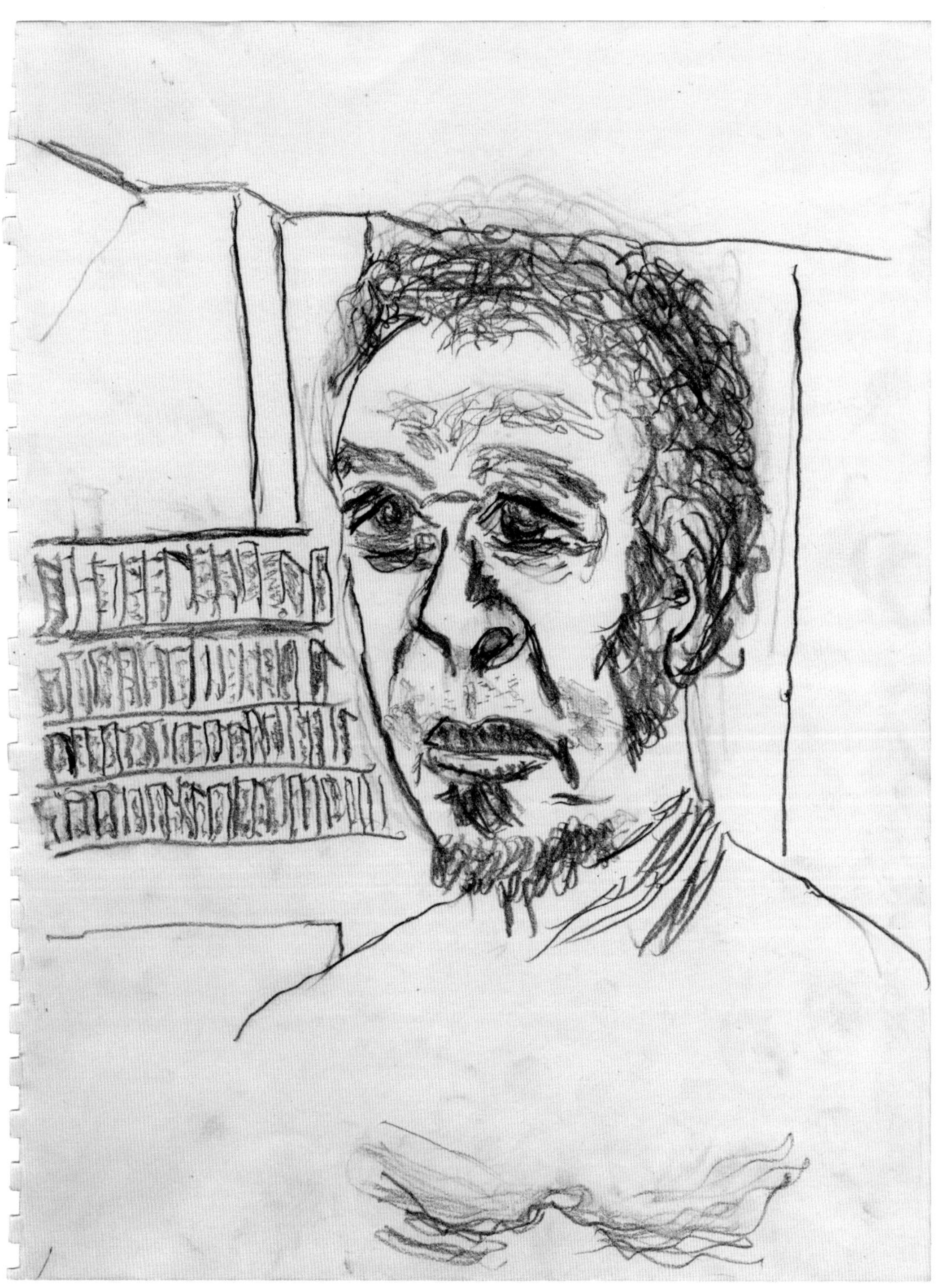

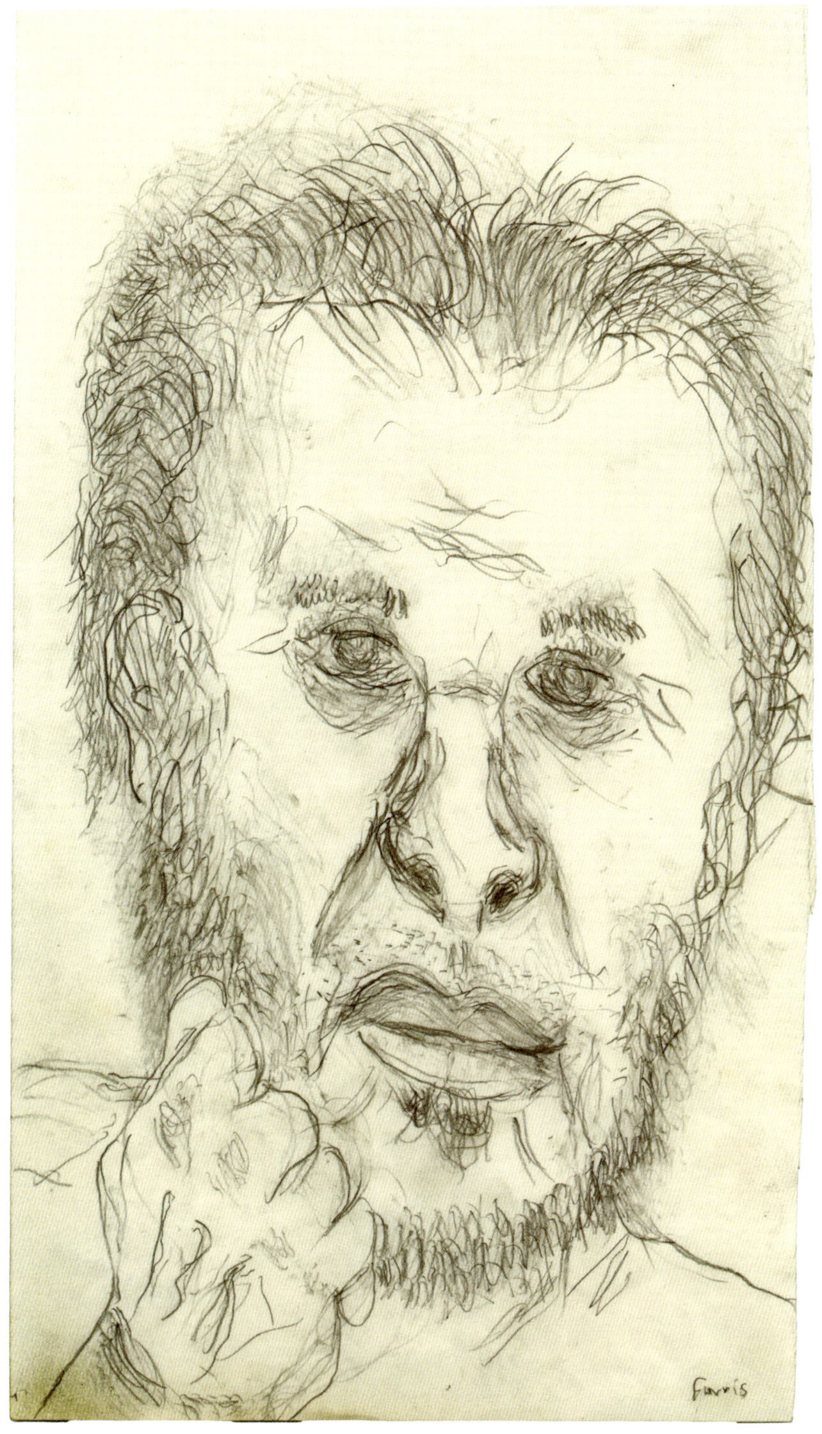

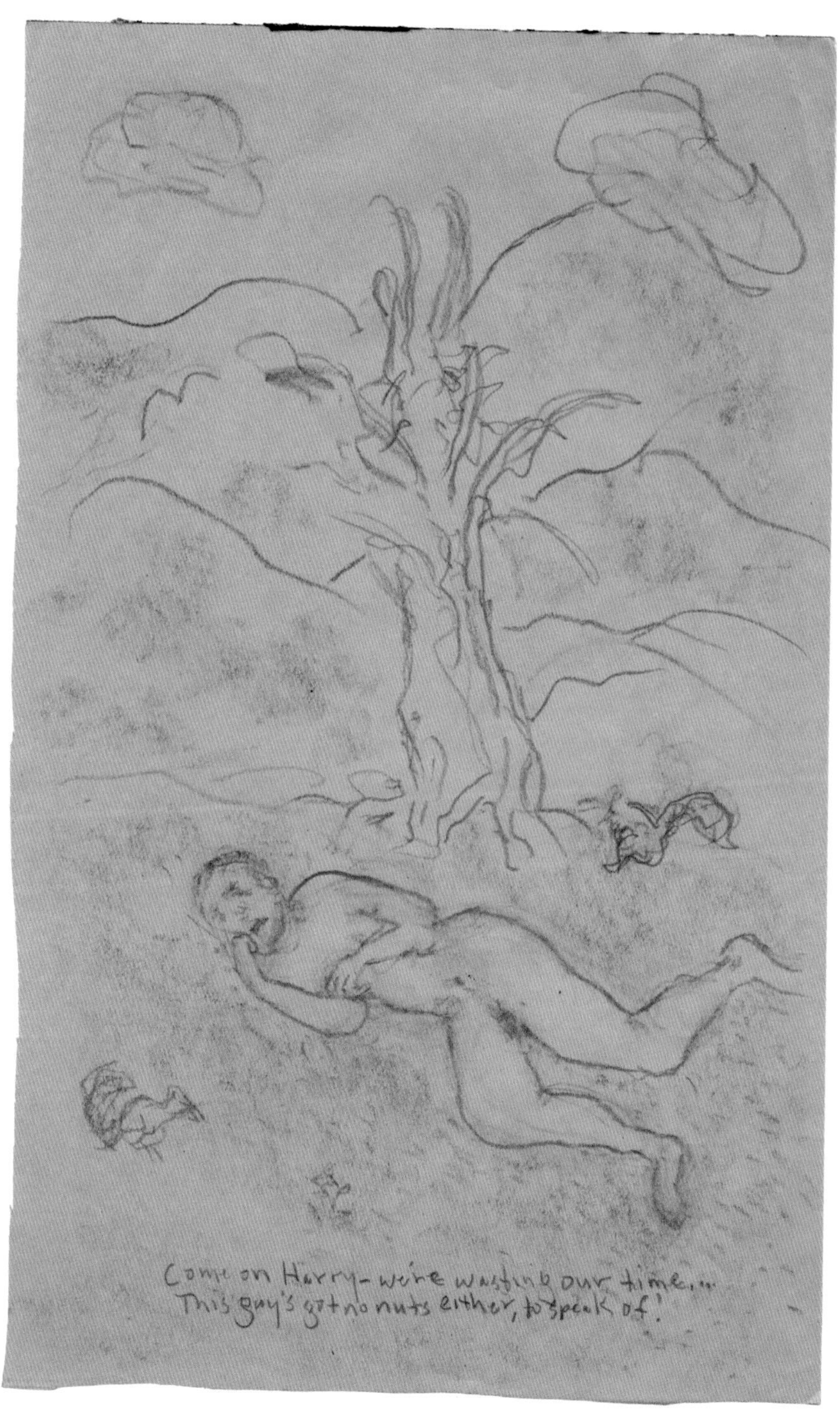
Come on Harry- we're wasting our time....
This guy's got no nuts either, to speak of!

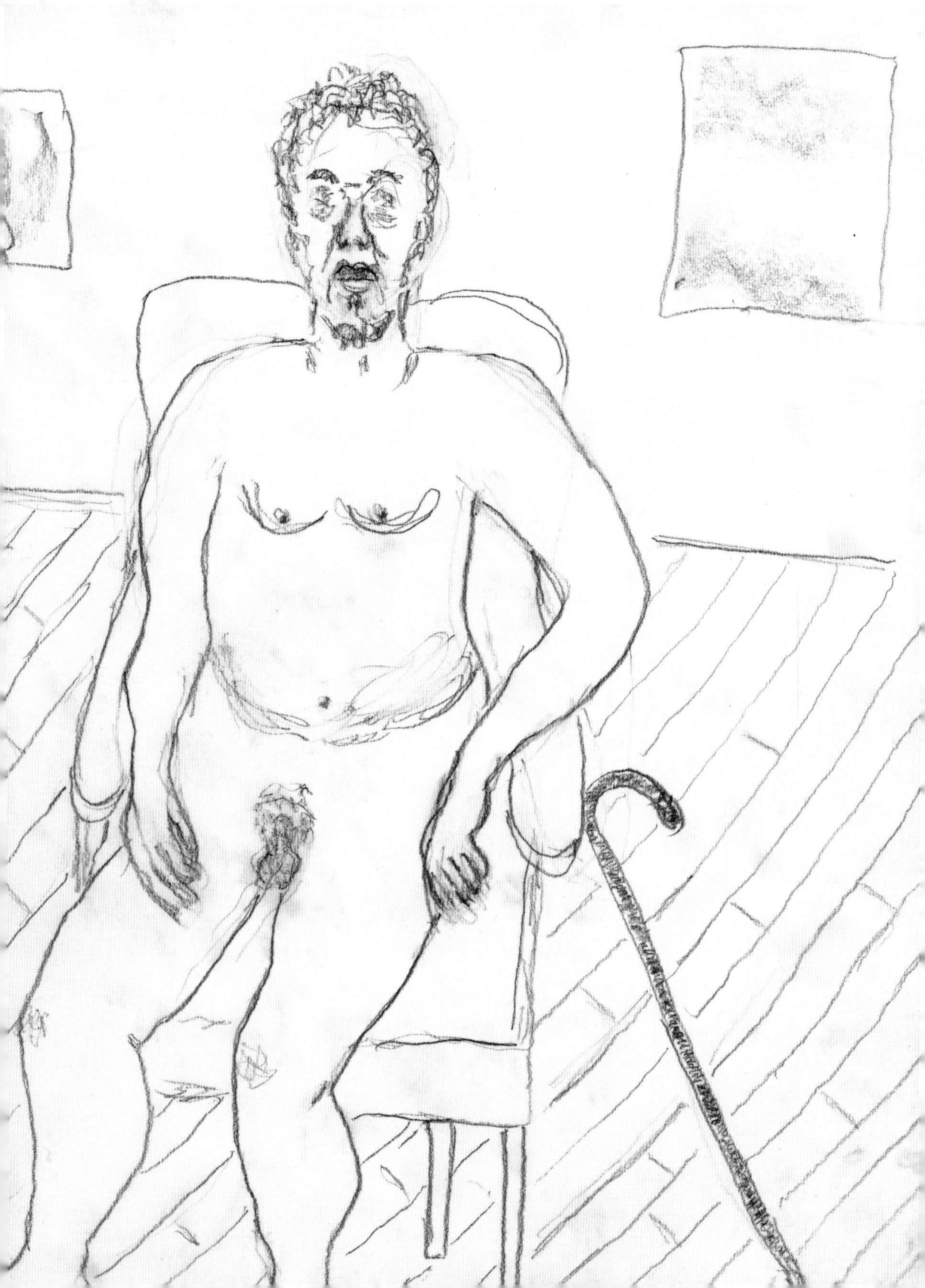

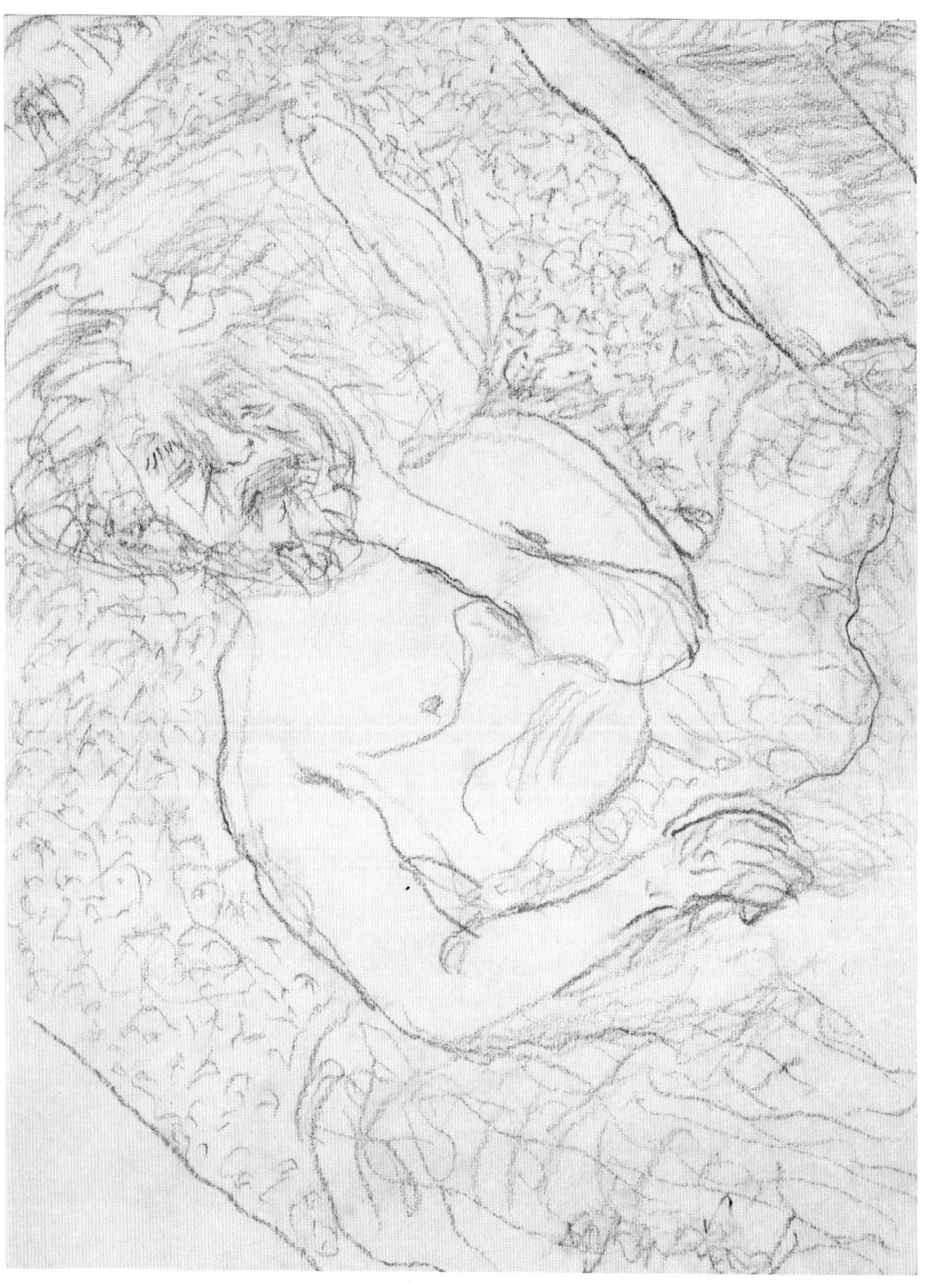

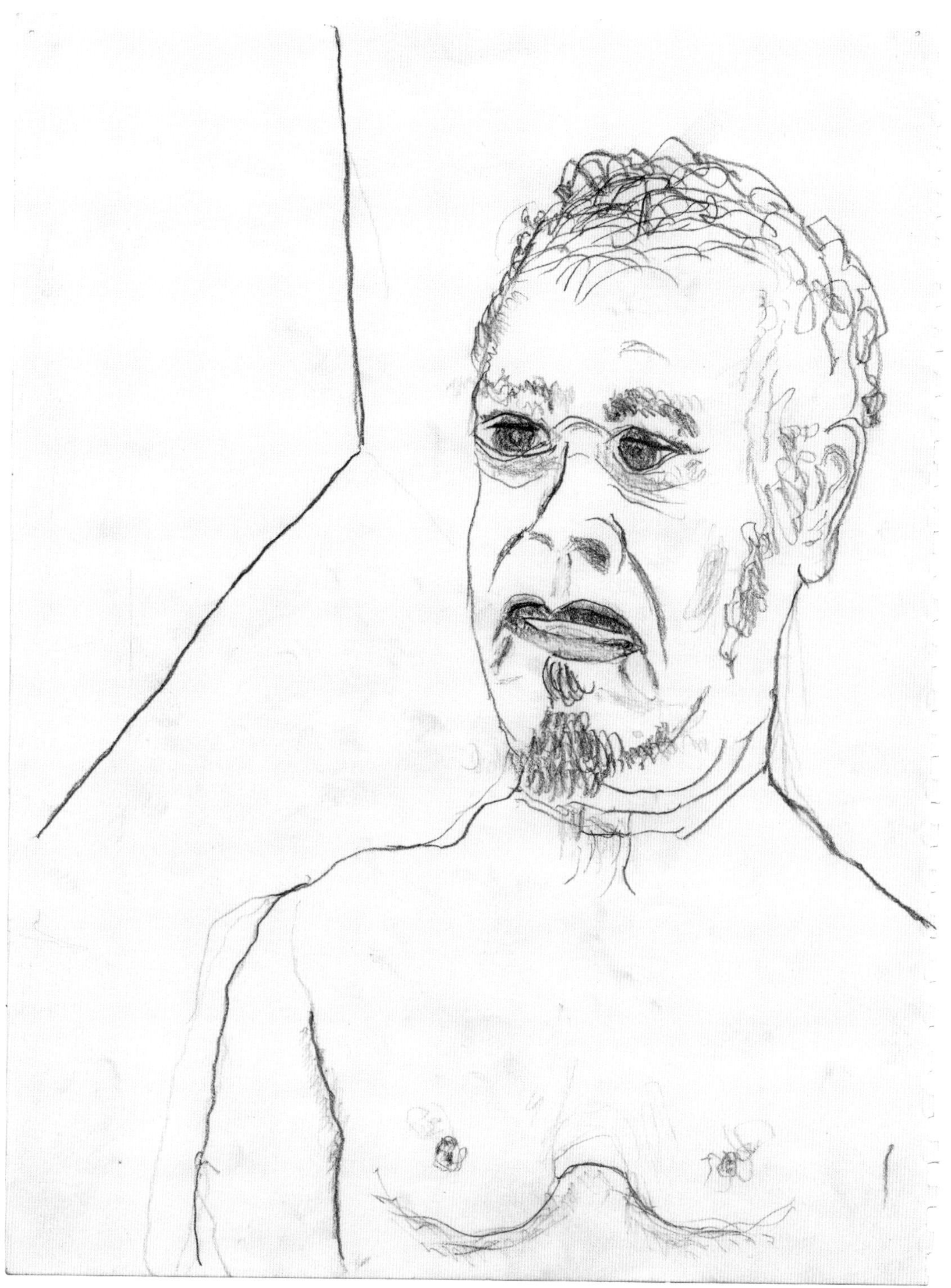

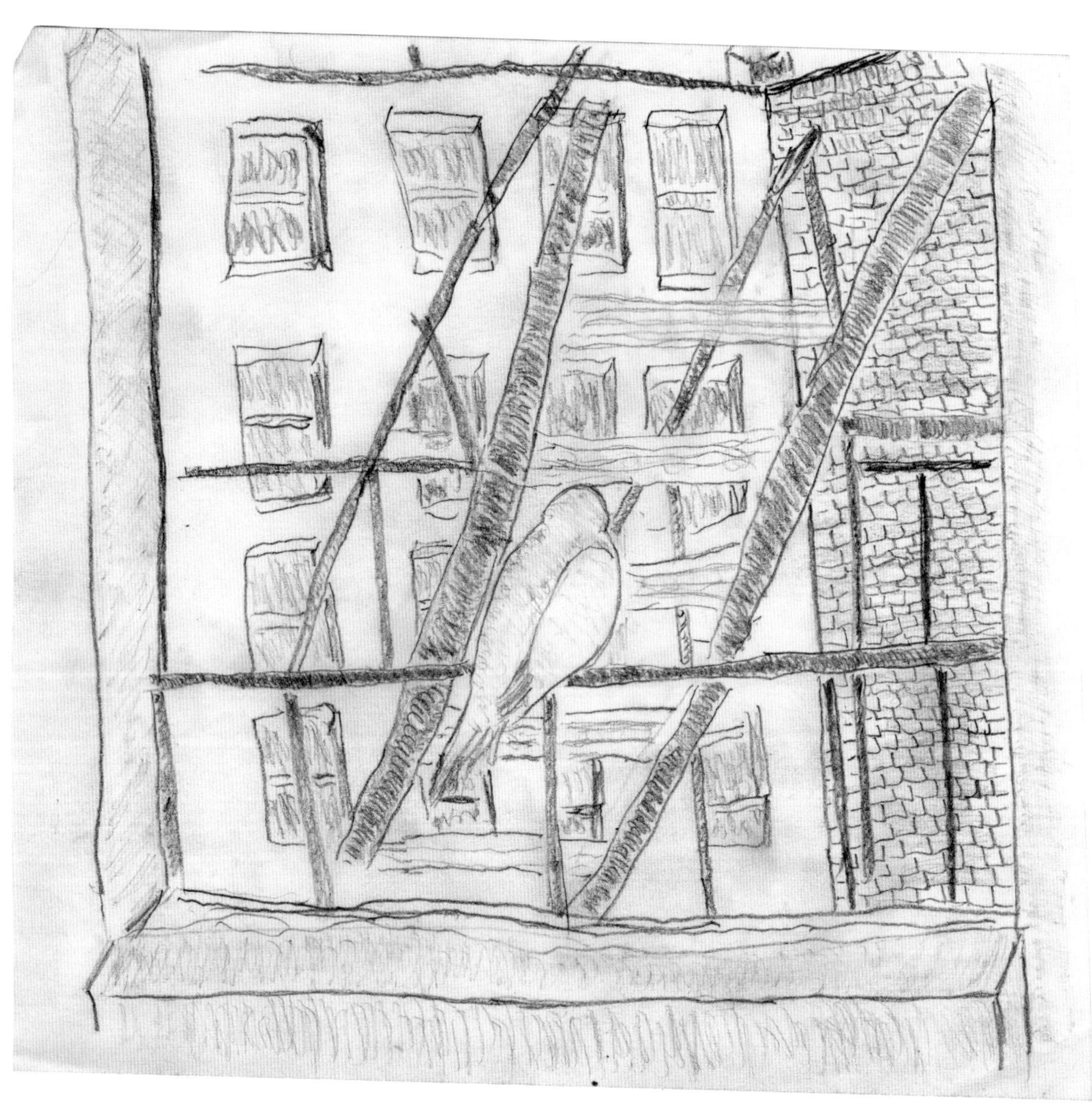

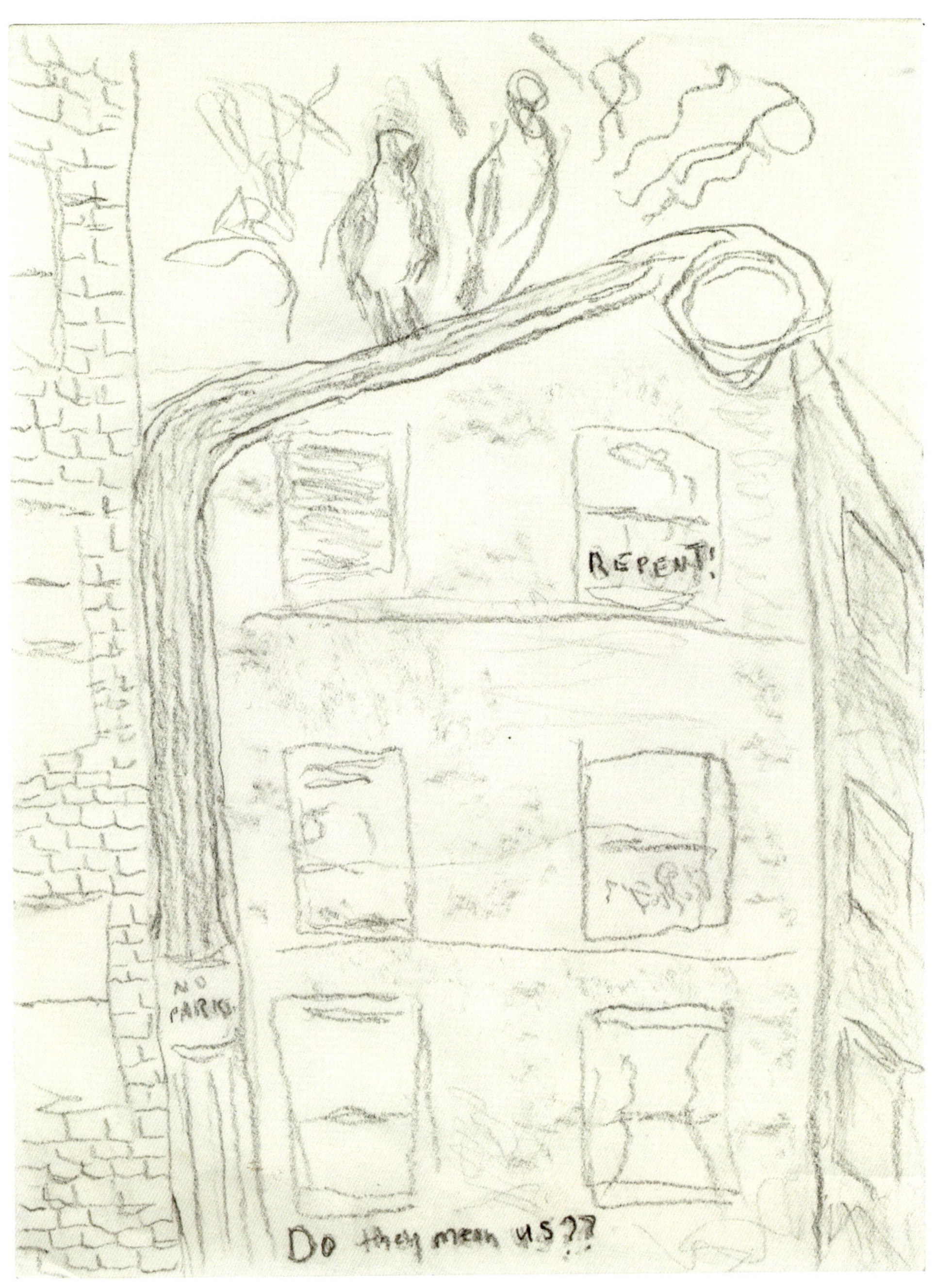
REPENT!
NO
PARK
Do they mean us??

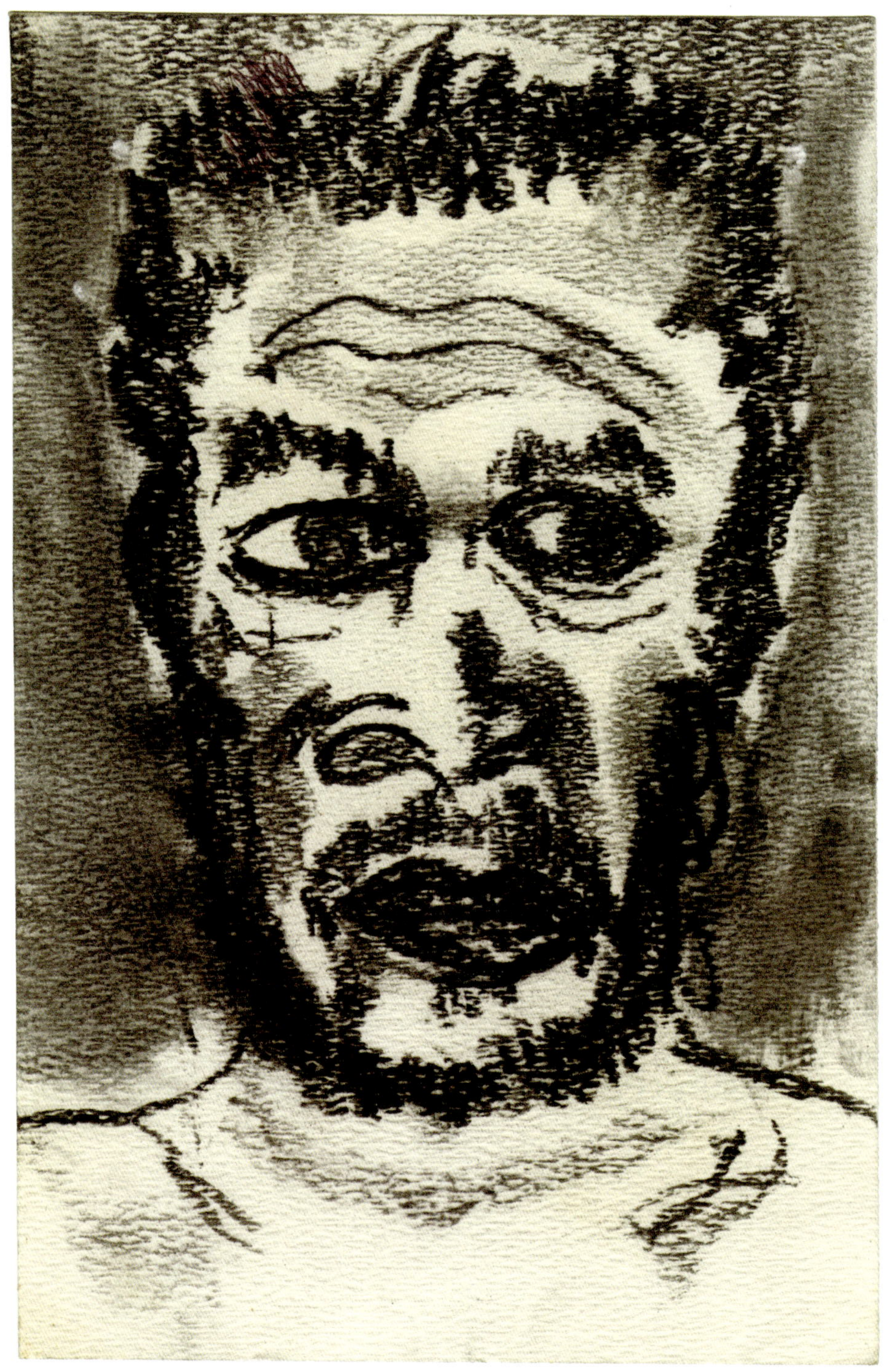

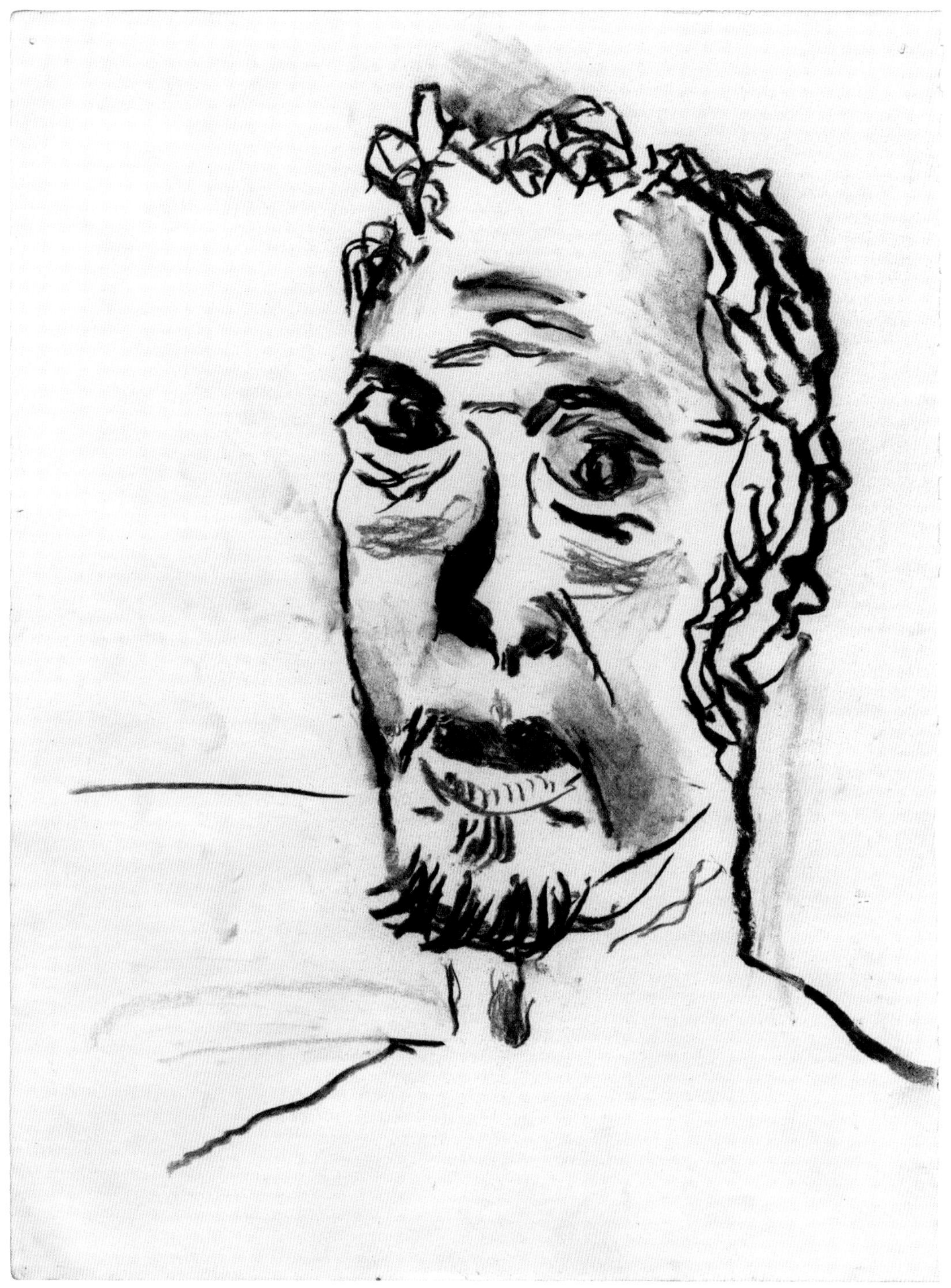

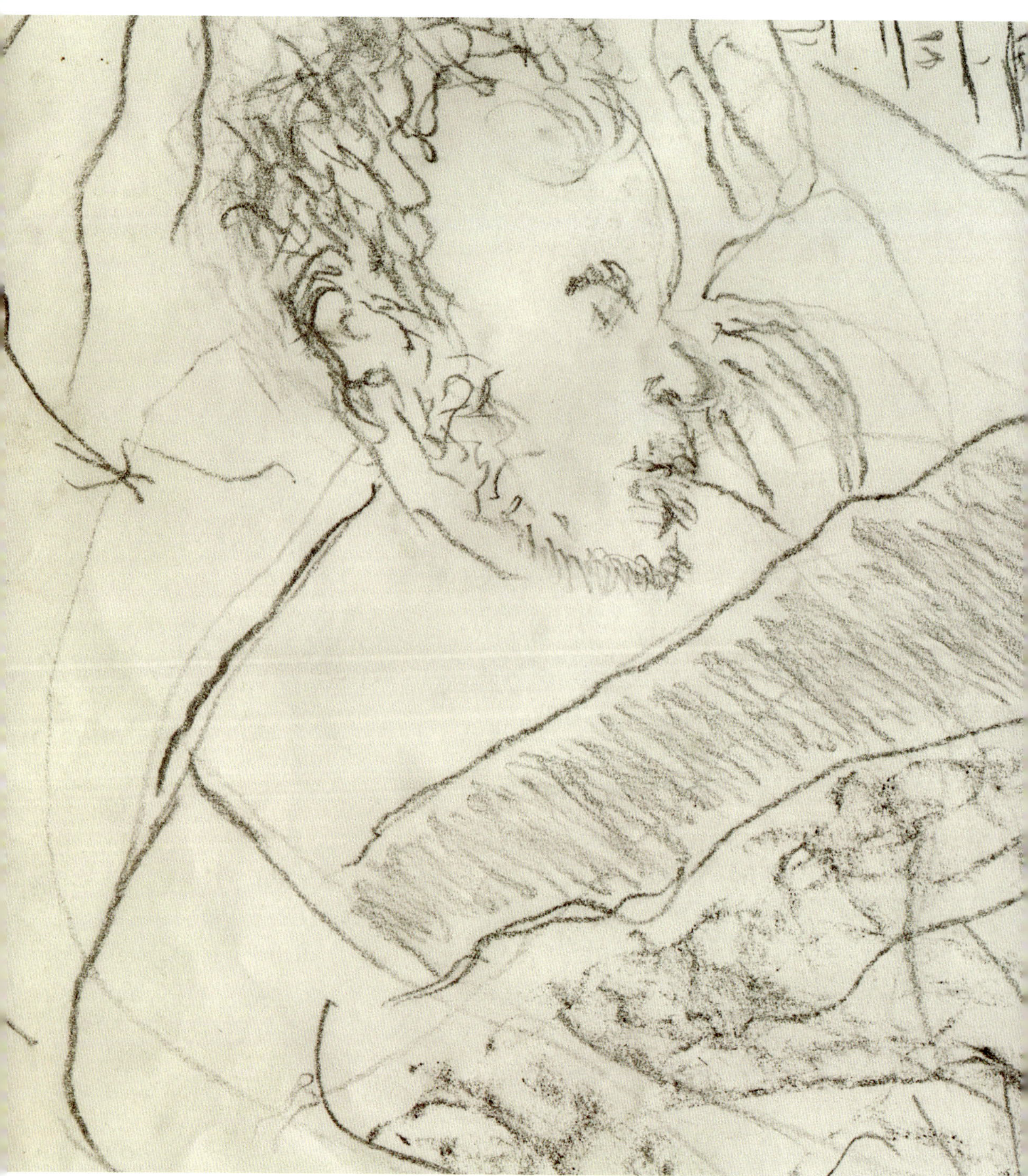

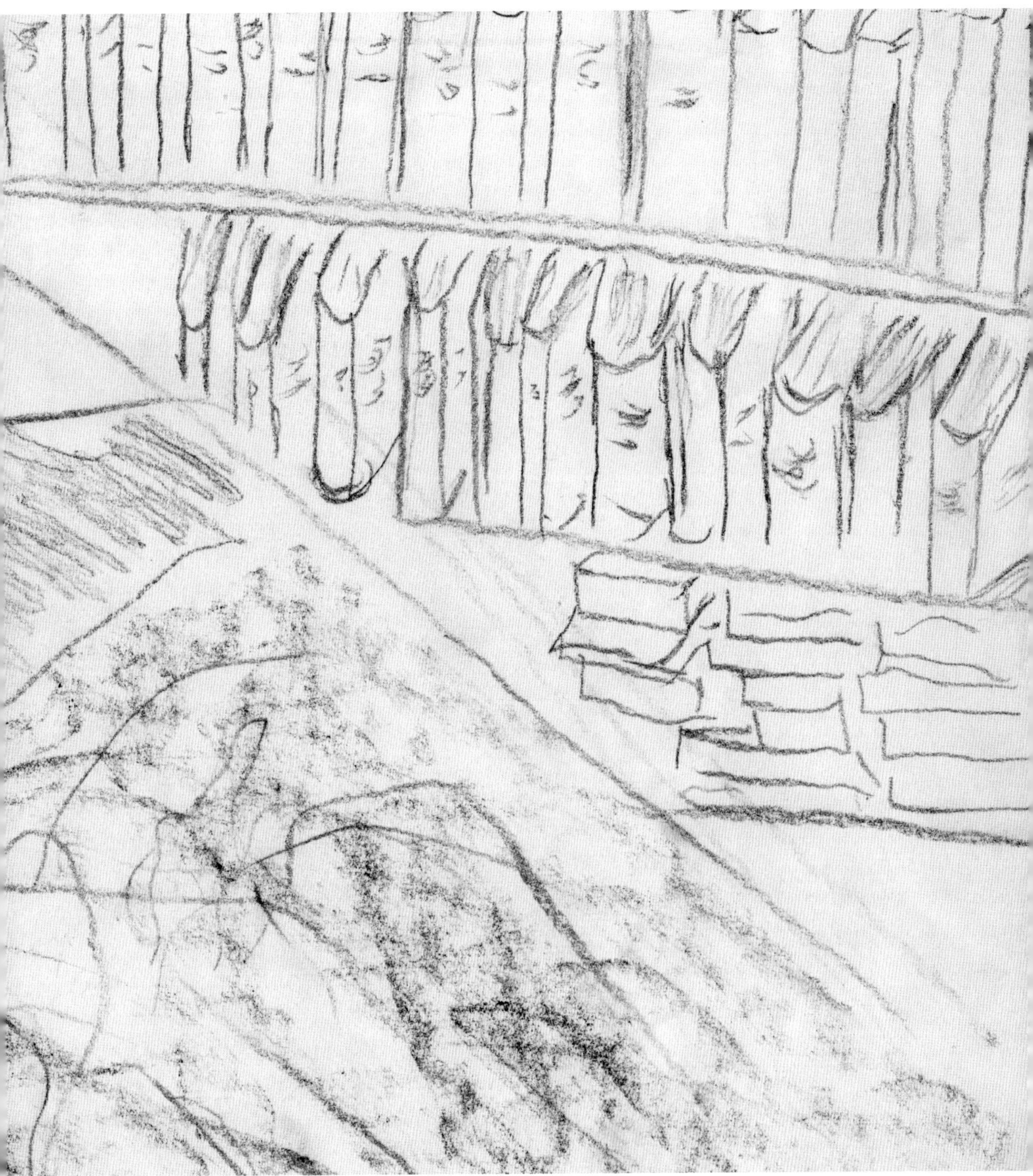

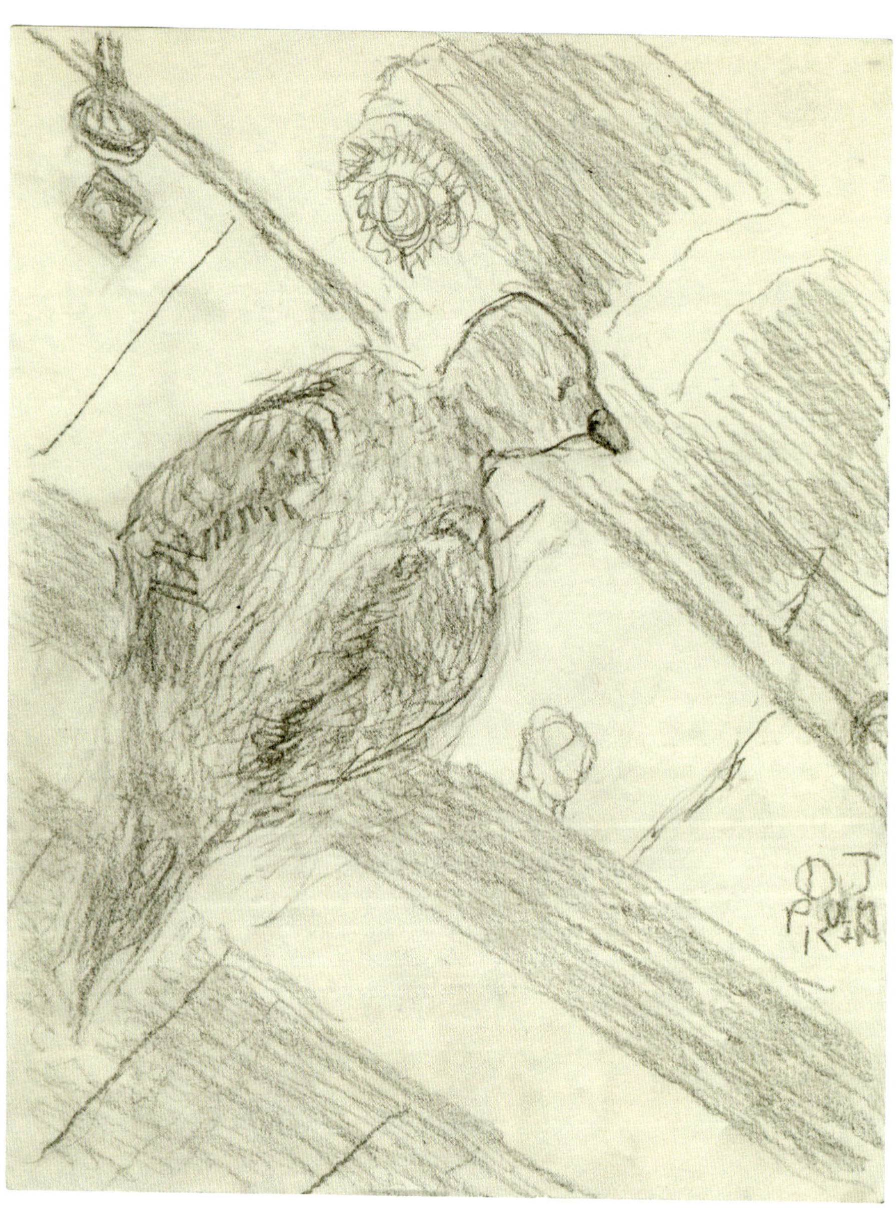

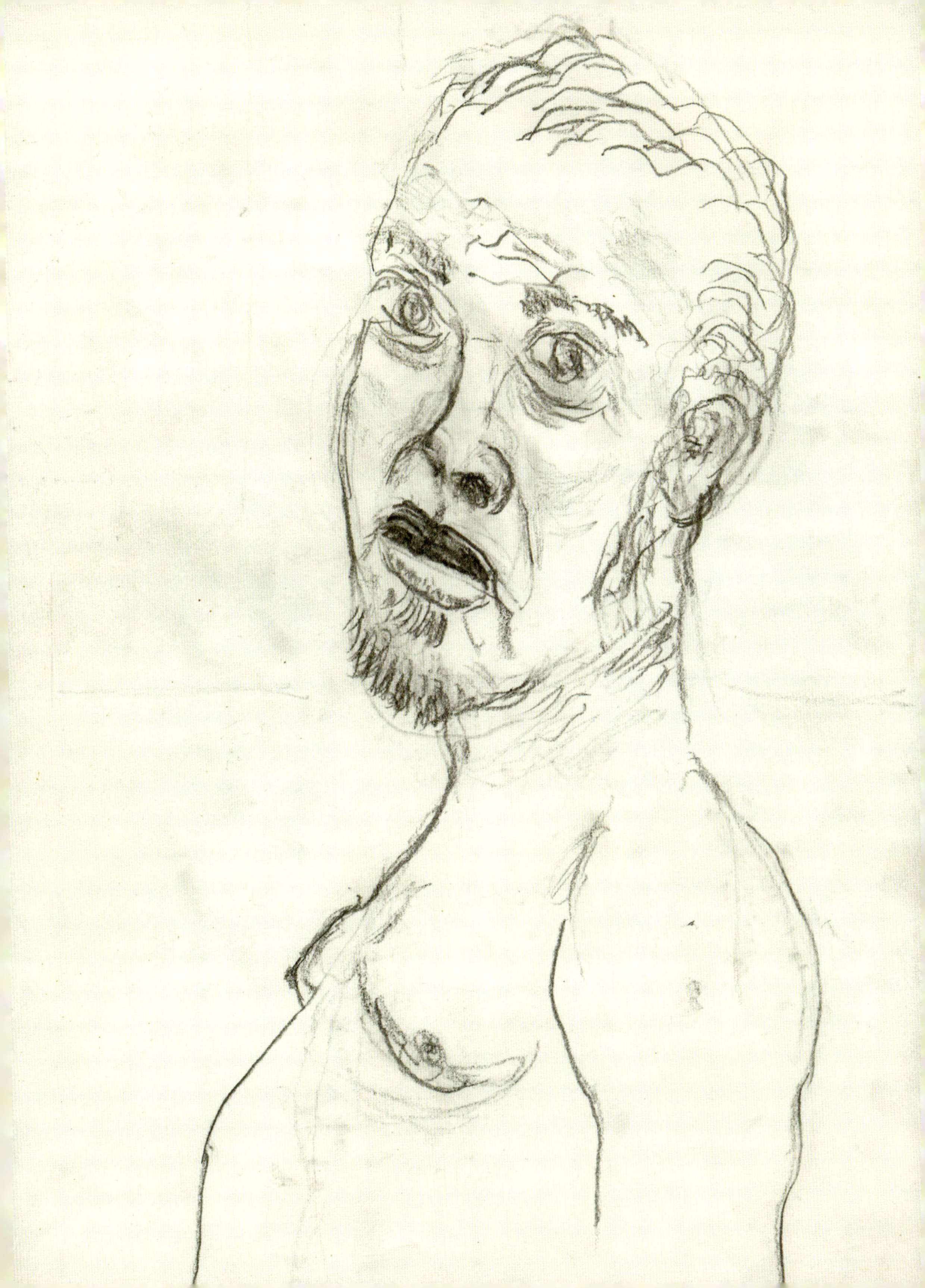

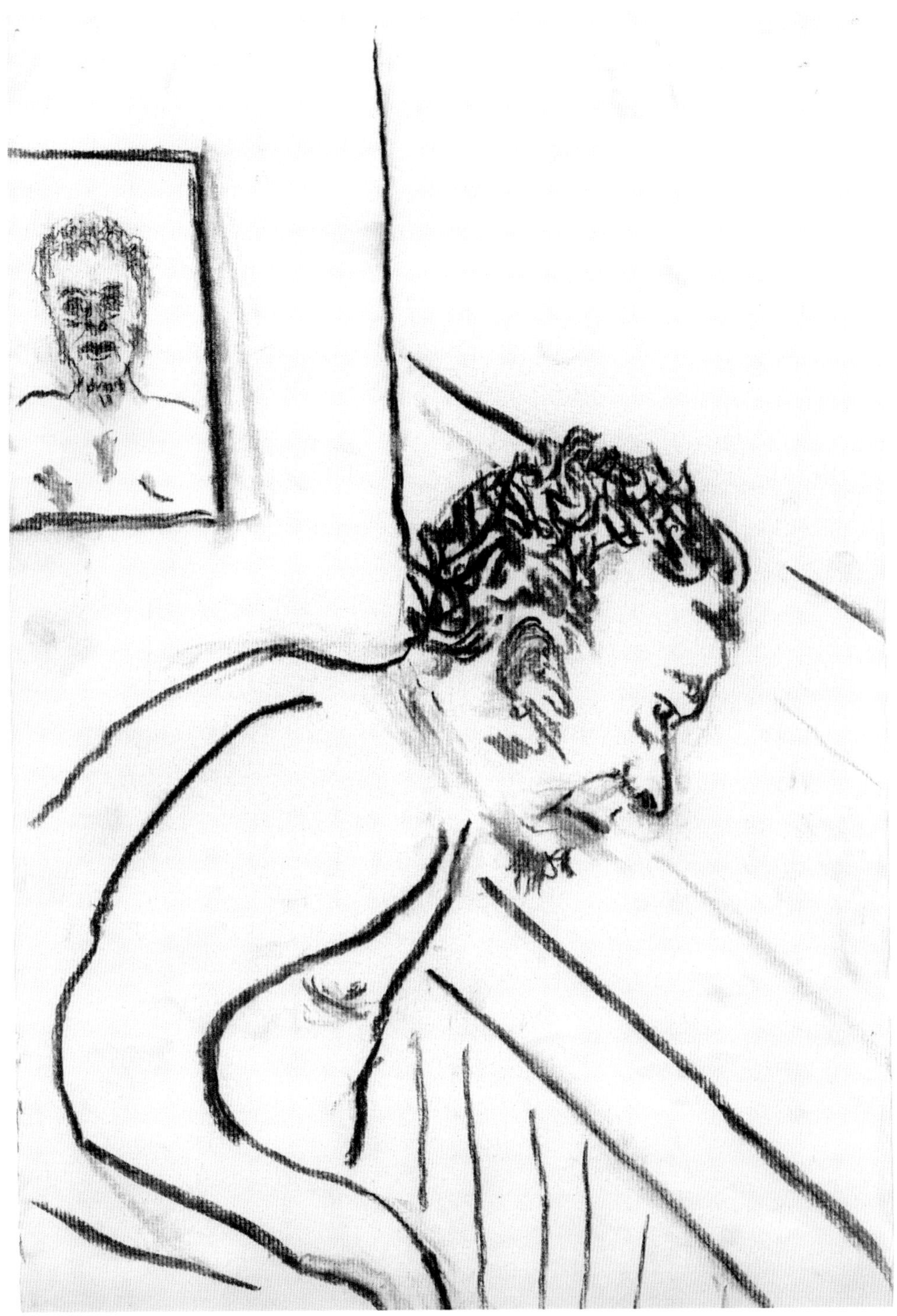

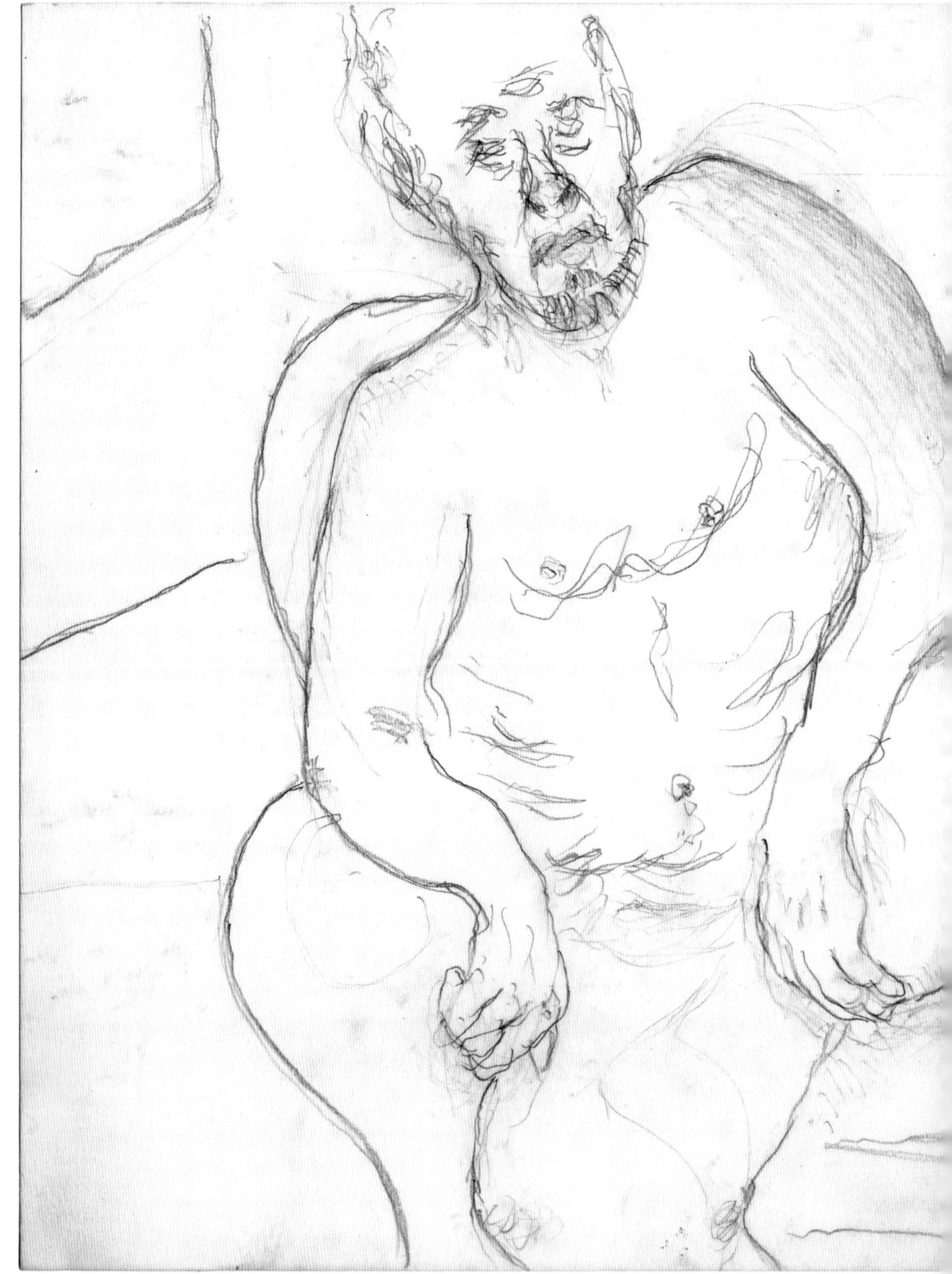

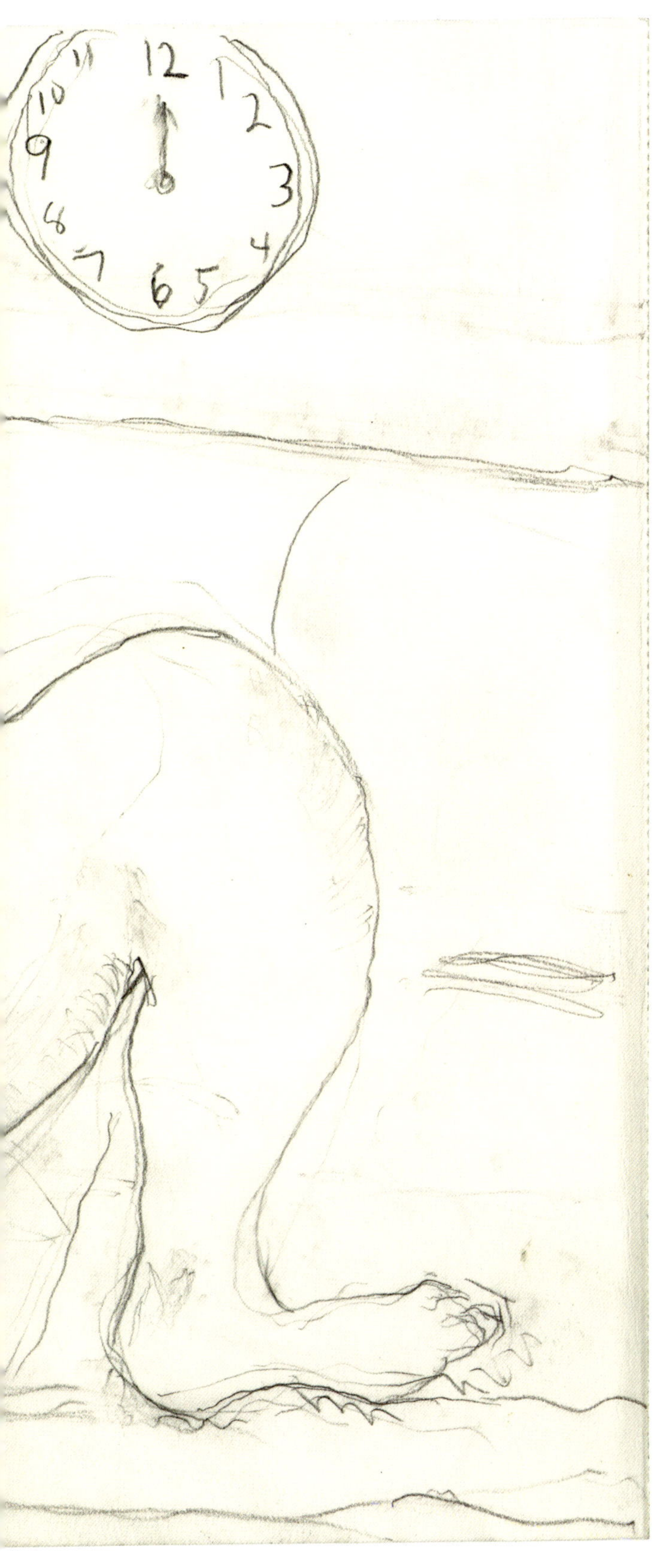
12
1
2
3
4
5
6
7
8
9
10
11

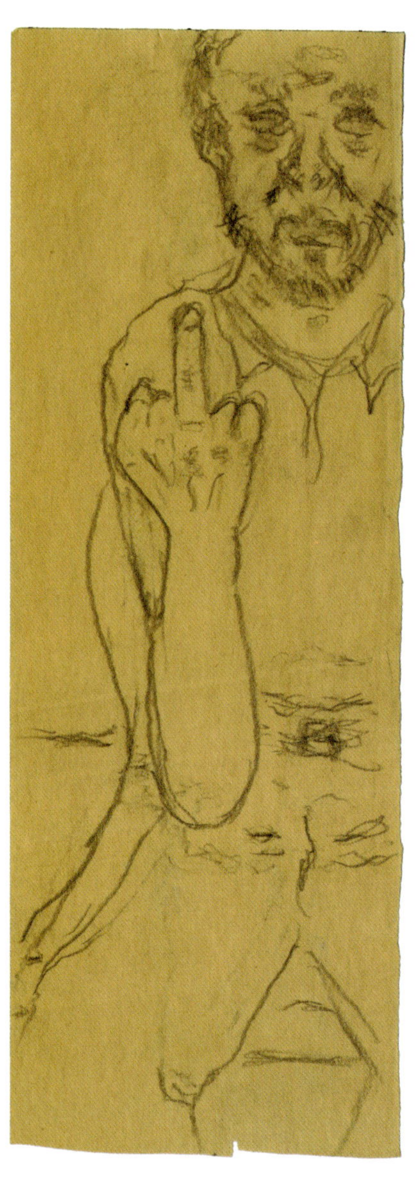

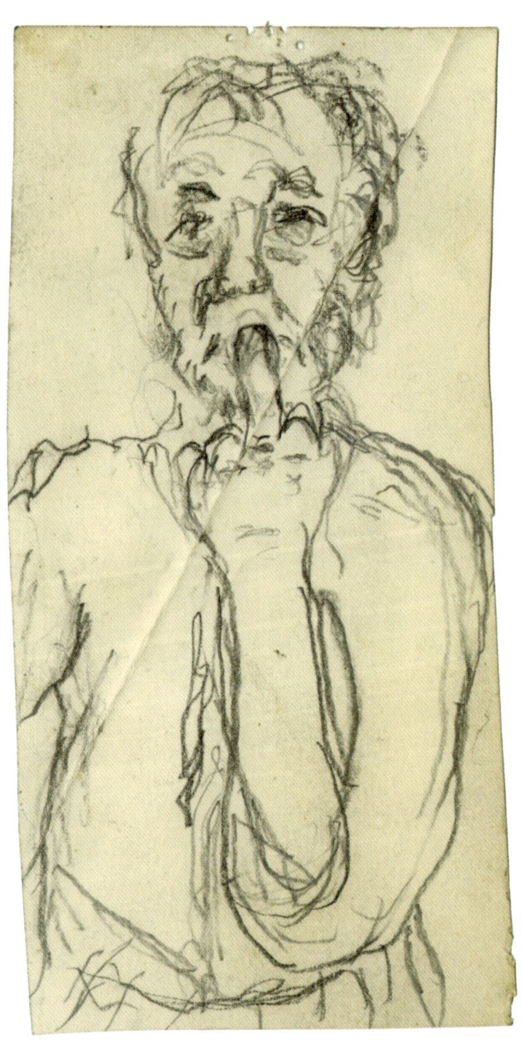

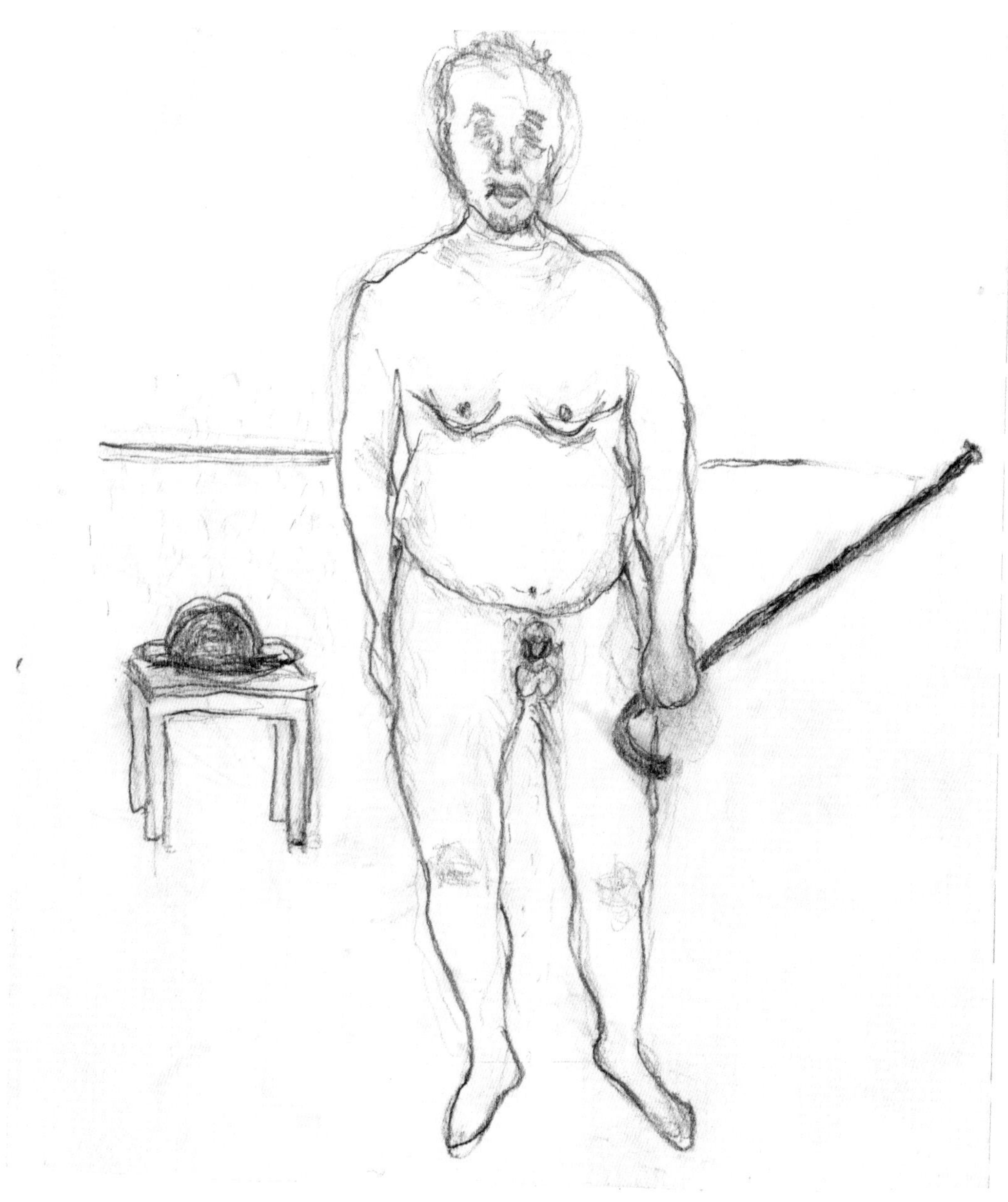

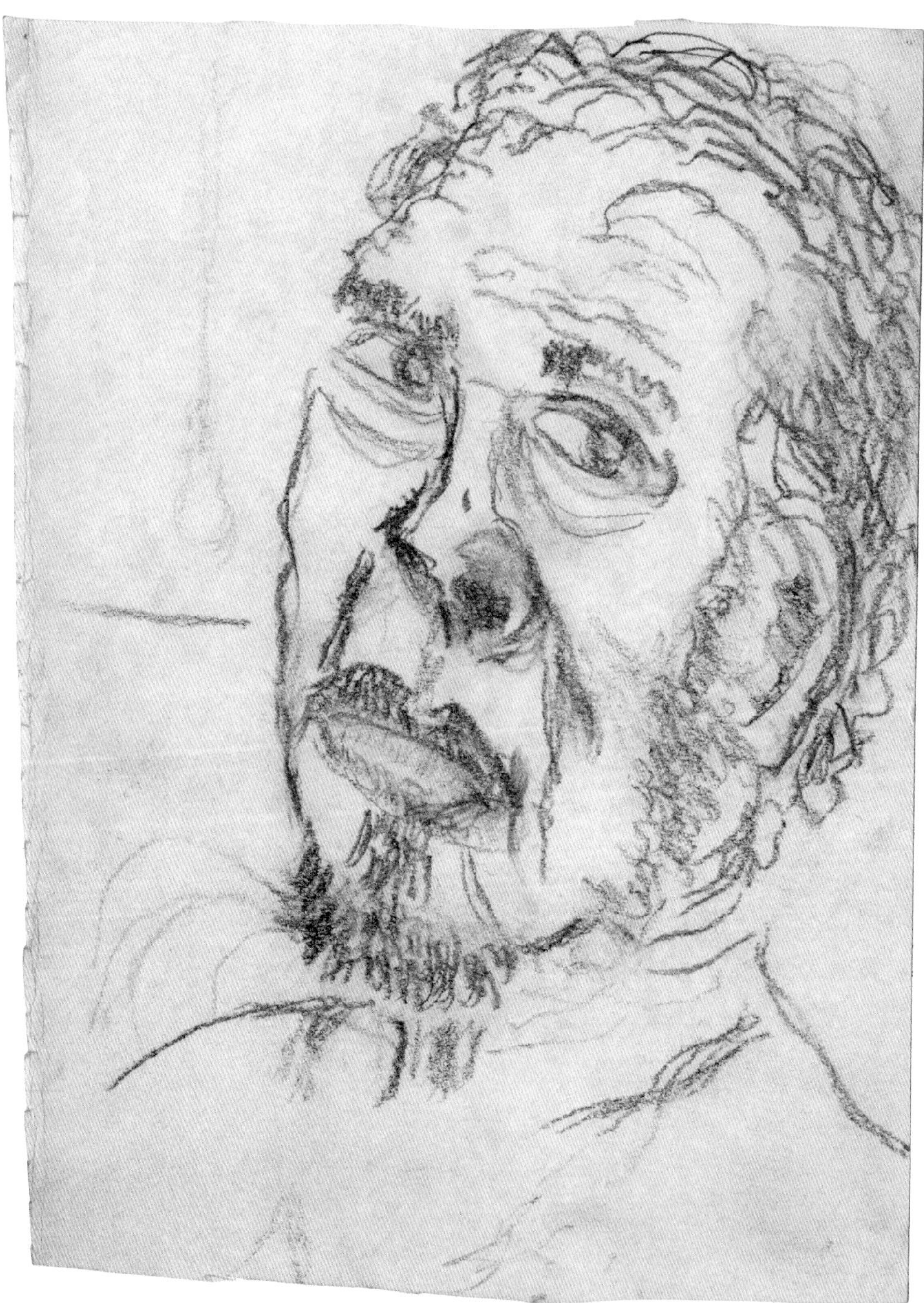

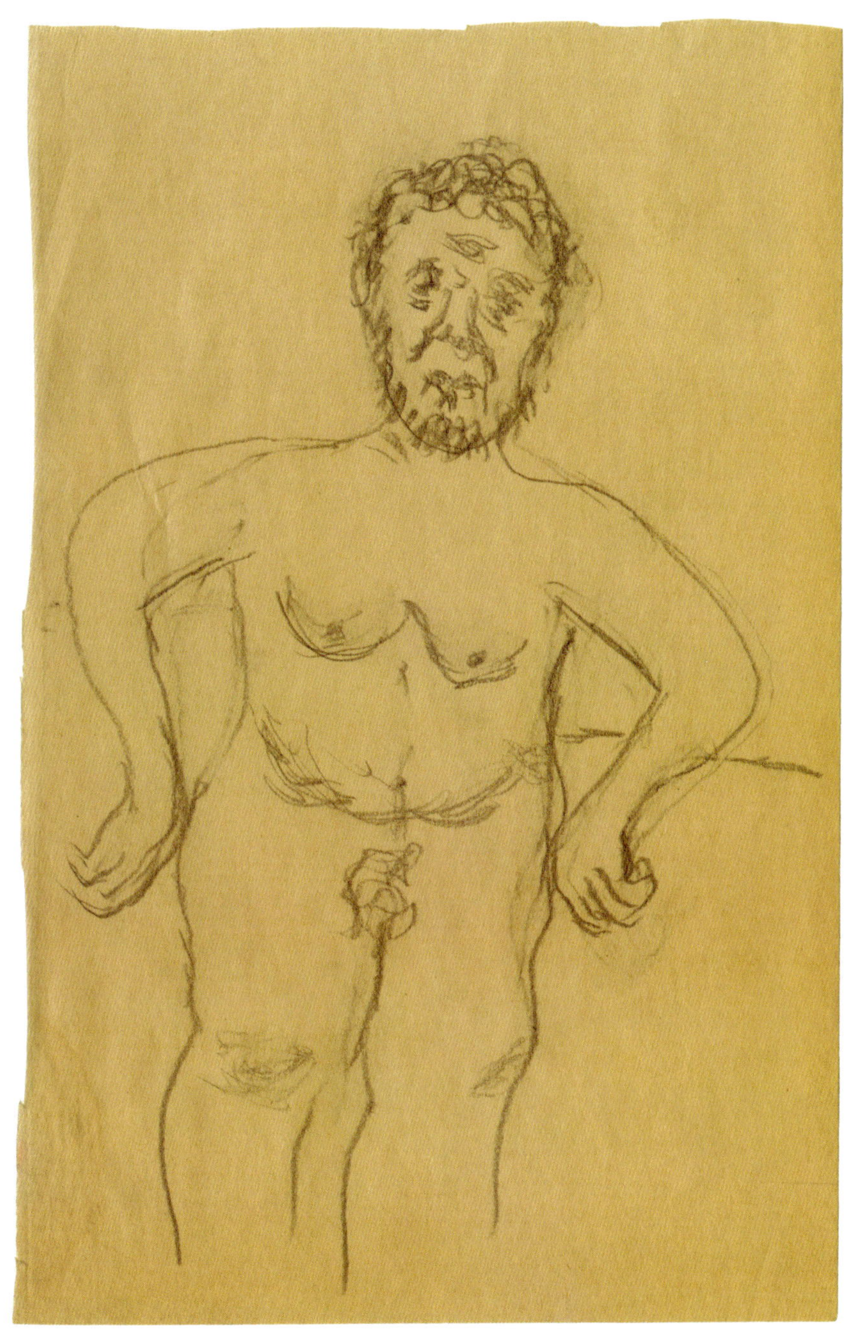

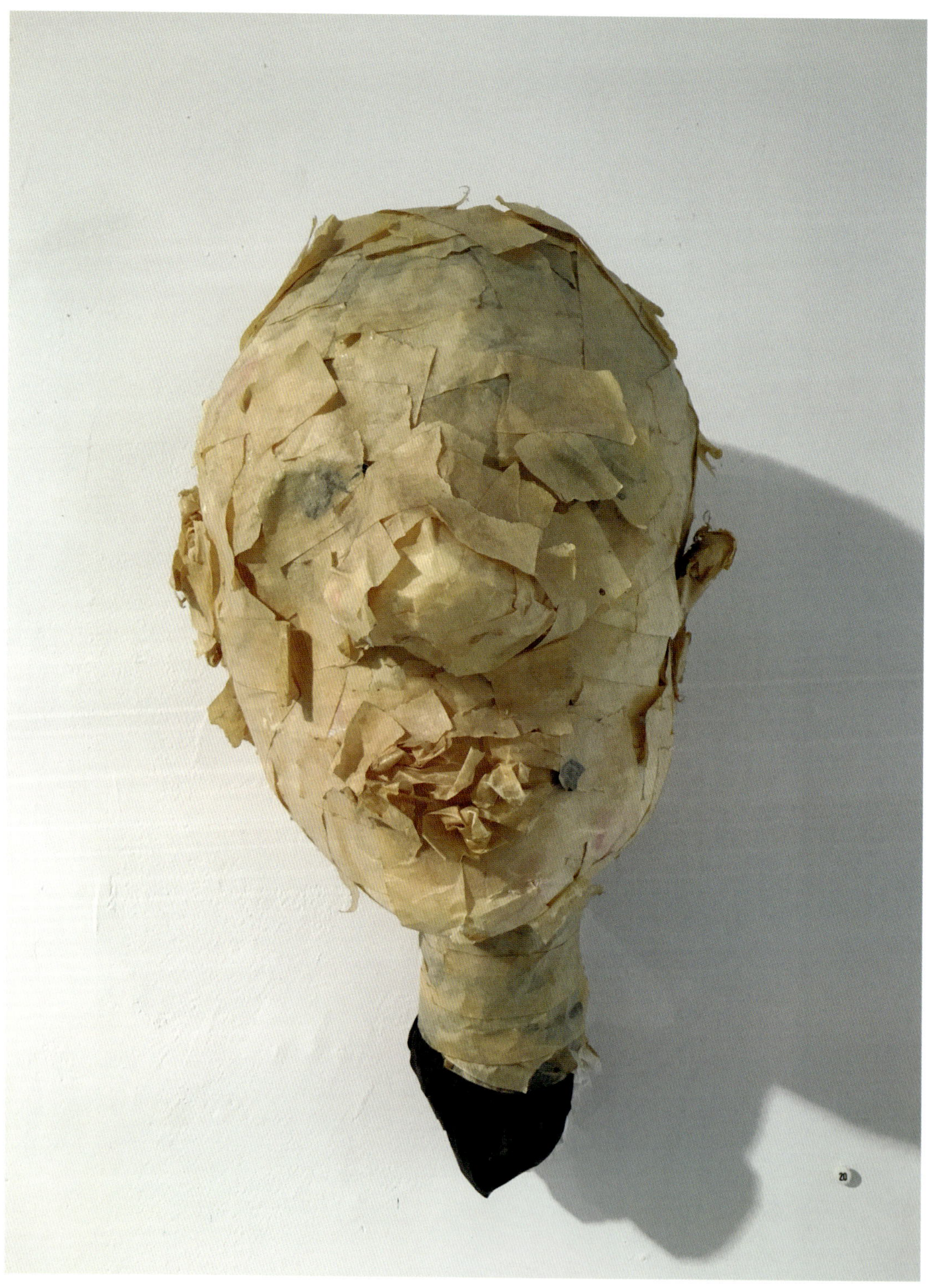

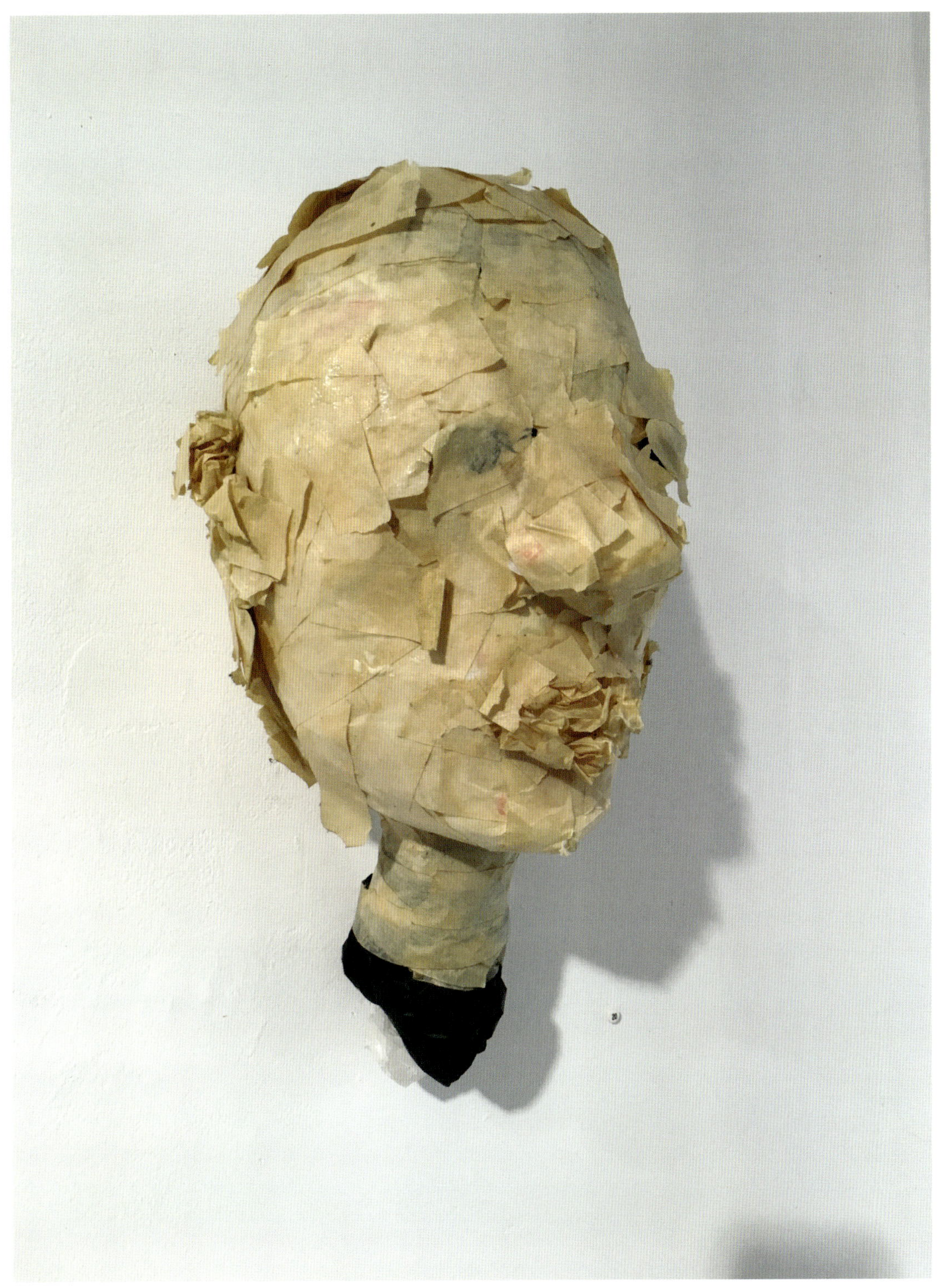

MORE FROM ARCHWAY EDITIONS

Archways 1
(edited by Chris Molnar and Nicodemus Nicoludis)
cokemachineglow: Writing Around Music 2005-2015
(edited by Clayton Purdom)
Claire Donato - *Kind Mirrors, Ugly Ghosts*
Gabriel Kruis - *Acid Virga*
Brantly Martin - *Highway B: Horrorfest*
NDA: An Autofiction Anthology
(edited by Caitlin Forst)
Alice Notley - *Runes and Chords*
Ishmael Reed - *Life Among the Aryans*
Ishmael Reed - *The Haunting of Lin-Manuel Miranda*
Ishmael Reed - *The Slave Who Loved Caviar*
Mike Sacks - *Randy & Stinker Lets Loose*
Paul Schrader - *First Reformed*
Stacy Szymaszek - *Famous Hermits*
Erin Taylor - *Bimboland*
charles theonia - *Gay Heaven is a Dance Floor but I Can't Relax*
Unpublishable
(edited by Chris Molnar and Etan Nechin)
Lindsey Webb - *Plat*

Forthcoming
Afsana Mousavi - *Love Story*
Christopher Coe - *Such Times*
Olivia Kan-Sperling - *Little Pink Book*
The Mystery of Perception: a conversation with Lynne Tillman
(edited by Taylor Lewandowski)
Chris Molnar - *Heaven's Oblivion*
Paul Schrader - *Hardcore*

Archway Editions is a literary imprint of indie art book publishing company **powerHouse Books**, and is distributed to the trade by Simon & Schuster; our books can be found in fine indie bookshops around the world, or Amazon if you must.

To learn more about **Archway Editions**, please visit here:

...and stop by our sister imprints **powerHouse Books**:

...and **POW! Kids Books**:

For trade queries, visit Simon & Schuster:

Send us love letters to:

Archway Editions
c/o POWERHOUSE Arena
32 Adams Street
Brooklyn, NY 11201

JOHN FARRIS was the author of the novel *The Ass's Tale* (Autonomedia, 2010) and the poetry collection *It's Not About Time* (Fly By Night Press, 1993). He was a fundamental part of the Downtown literary and jazz scenes, a poet, playwright and novelist, bodyguard to Malcolm X, associate of many figures and organizations (whether living under the Living Theatre or on Ornette Coleman's couch), and a genius of the writing life.